AN INTRODUCTION TO BUSINESS CALCULATIONS
THROUGH ASSIGNMENTS

MACMILLAN TEXTS FOR BUSINESS STUDIES

Joseph Chilver: An Introduction to Business Calculations through Assignments

Joseph Chilver: Introducing Business Studies: A Case-Study and Assignment Approach

Forthcoming

Lysbeth A. Woolcott and Wendy R. Unwin: Communication for Business and Secretarial Students, *Second Edition*

James Dunbar-Brunton: The Law and the Individual, *Revised Edition*

An Introduction to Business Calculations through Assignments

JOSEPH CHILVER

B.Sc. Econ. (Hons.) Lond., A.I.B. (and Trustee Dip.) A.I.P.M., A.M.B.I.M.
Dorset Institute of Higher Education

First published 1979 by
THE MACMILLAN PRESS LTD
London and Basingstoke
Associated companies in Delhi Dublin
Hong Kong Johannesburg Lagos Melbourne
New York Singapore and Tokyo

Typeset by
CAMBRIAN TYPESETTERS
and printed in Great Britain by
Unwin Brothers Limited
The Gresham Press Old Woking Surrey

British Library Cataloguing in Publication Data

Chilver, Joseph
An introduction to business calculations through assignments. – (Macmillan texts for business studies).
1. Business mathematics – Problems, exercises, etc.
I. Title
513'. 93'076 HF5695

ISBN 0–333–25692–1

Contents

Preface ix

1 The Basic Techniques 1
Fractions 1
Decimals 7
Percentages 12
Averages 20
Visual Presentation 22

2 The Assignments 28
Assignment No.
1 Festival of Flowers 29
2 Boating Holidays 31
3 Sunnybrook Farm 34
4 The Belvedere Hotel 35
5 The Booksellers 38
6 V.G. Antiques 41
7 Vivian's Van Hire 43
8 Contessa Glassware 45
9 Footwear Fashions 48
10 Shane's Reproductions 50
11 The Guys and Dolls Disco 52
12 Buyrite Supermarkets 54
13 The Stratford Beacon 56
14 Slattery Mirrors 59
15 Swiss Breakfast Food 61
16 Burton United 63
17 The Surf-skaters 65
18 The Railway Time-table 67
19 Stock Control 68
20 Nevada Night Ride 72

21 Spreadeagle Sports 75
22 Hire-purchase 77
23 Household Expenses 81
24 The Sales Representatives 82
25 Jamboree Jars Ltd 86
26 Alpha Motors 88
27 Christmas Crackers 90
28 Walls & Daws (Estate Agents) 92
29 Seasonal Demands 94
30 Chocolate Bars 97
31 Orion Insurance 100
32 Crampton Electrics 101
33 Amateur Dramatics 104
34 Wedding Bells 107
35 Sam's Place 110
36 The Legatees 113
37 The Gas Board 115
38 French Leave 118
39 The Continental Tour 121
40 Costs and Returns 122

3 Speed and Accuracy Tests 125
Percentages, Fractions and Decimals 125
Pick the Winner 127
Time Trial 128
Add and Check 129
Call, Copy and Add 130
Multiply and Subtract 132
Divide and Add 133
Meter Readings 134
Foreign Exchange Handicap I 136
Foreign Exchange Handicap II 137
Convert and Compare 140
Averages 141
The Gladiators I 142
The Gladiators II 143
Debits and Credits I 145
Debits and Credits II 146
The Satellite 147

4 Conventional Examination Work 149
Questions with workings 150
Questions to be worked 159
Business Education Council: Specimen Examination Paper 162

Appendix – Solutions 166

Preface

With the advent of the new Business Education Council (B.E.C.) courses an opportunity has been given to educationalists to review both their teaching material and the objectives of their courses. The approach adopted here is to provide a variety of new-look frameworks for a series of exercises appropriate to General Level and some first-year National Level Courses of the Business Education Council as well as the more familiar courses related to the examinations set by the Royal Society of Arts and the London Chamber of Commerce and Industry. The aim is to catch the imagination of students on the threshold of a business career, at the same time familiarising them with the sort of calculations they might expect to be confronted with in real-life business. Personal involvement is the key-note and every attempt has been made to conform to the new B.E.C. philosophy. Each of the main exercises is followed by questions for group discussion, and the exercises are framed in the form of assignments which are related to real-life events.

The learning process starts with an introductory section on 'The Basic Techniques' but the teaching process continues throughout the text and could be described from the student's point of view as a programme of Learning through Involvement.

The effect of this new approach to the teaching of business calculations should be to make the work more interesting and examination-taking less painful. Students will be able to put the theory to the test when they come to Section 4, which is devoted to conventional examination work.

Where tutors find that students have serious deficiencies, a diagnostic test could be given to reveal detailed weaknesses as a prelude to intensive remedial work. But for all students the merit of clearly laid-out work and sufficient – though not excessive – explanations of the steps being pursued is worth emphasising, as is the value of good figures. Employers frequently complain of students being unable to produce a clear statement of an argument or an account, and every attempt should be made to remedy these defects if, and when, they appear.

The characters and companies referred to are wholly fictitious, though it is hoped the situations described are such as might be found in real-life business.

My thanks go to Norman Aslett, F.C.A., A.C.C.A., A.C.I.S.; my colleague at the Dorset Institute of Higher Education, who kindly read the script for me and made many useful suggestions for improvement.

Joseph Chilver

1 The Basic Techniques

Many of the skills you will be expected to develop through your work in this book will be acquired during the various Assignments which follow in the main body of the text – in Section 2. However, it is necessary for you to have a grasp of certain basic techniques before you progress to the Assignments. In this first section, therefore, we shall concentrate on the vital areas of fractions, decimals and percentages. We shall also pay attention to the subject of averages and, finally, look at ways in which business data might be represented visually. These techniques will then be developed further and treated at greater length during the course of the Assignments and other exercises which follow.

FRACTIONS

A fraction is a part of something. We may express that part as a 'vulgar fraction', i.e. ½ or ¼ or $^1/_3$ etc. or as a 'decimal fraction', i.e. $^1/_{10}$, $^1/_{100}$, $^1/_{1000}$, when they are written

0.1 0.01 0.001

One way of remembering how to deal with fractions is to think about an orange. Cut the orange in half (mentally at least) and then cut one of the halves into half again. What is a half of a half of an orange? The answer is a quarter.

How can we show this mathematically?

½ of ½ is written ½ x ½
and ½ x ½ of an orange = ¼

How do we arrive at that?

We multiply the two figures on the top line, i.e.
$1 \times 1 = 1$
and we multiply the two figures on the bottom line, i.e.
$2 \times 2 = 4$

To take a slightly more complicated example:

What is $^2/_3$ of $^3/_4$? Answer = $\frac{\overset{1}{\cancel{2}}}{\underset{1}{\cancel{3}}} \times \frac{\overset{1}{\cancel{3}}}{\underset{2}{\cancel{4}}} = \frac{1}{2}$

Next time you have an orange to eat you can confirm that the above calculation is correct. Cut it into quarters, and eat one of the quarters. There are three quarters left ($^3/_4$). Eat one of these and you have two-thirds ($^2/_3$) of the three quarters ($^3/_4$) left. What is two-thirds of three-quarters ($^2/_3 \times ^3/_4$)?

Whenever you are dealing with fractions you can multiply or divide any figure above the line so long as you do the same thing below the line. That is why we were able to cancel out figures – above and below the line – in the last example.

Adding or subtracting fractions usually requires this treatment. Consider first a problem.

How can one deduct $^5/_8$ from $^3/_4$?

It is like having to deduct sheep from goats. One can deduct sheep from sheep. One can deduct goats from goats. But one cannot deduct sheep from goats – or goats from sheep. We can call them both 'animals' and deduct animals from animals. In the question posed (deduct $^5/_8$ from $^3/_4$) we proceed by turning them into the 'same kind of thing': here we turn the $^3/_4$ into eighths = $^6/_8$. Now we can solve our problem:

$$^6/_8 - ^5/_8 = ^1/_8$$

Here are some more examples:

(i) $\frac{5}{6} - \frac{1}{2} = \frac{5}{6} - \frac{3}{6} = \frac{2}{6} = \frac{1}{3}$

(ii) $\frac{7}{12} + \frac{3}{4} = \frac{7}{12} + \frac{9}{12} = \frac{16}{12} = 1\frac{4}{12} = 1\frac{1}{3}$

(iii) $\frac{3}{8}$ of $\frac{5}{6} = \frac{\overset{1}{\cancel{3}}}{8} \times \frac{5}{\underset{2}{\cancel{6}}} = \frac{5}{16}$

When you cannot divide the top and bottom figures (the numerator and denominator respectively) any further, this becomes the final answer.

(iv) $\frac{5}{8}$ of $\frac{2}{15} = \frac{\overset{1}{\cancel{5}}}{\underset{4}{\cancel{8}}} \times \frac{\overset{1}{\cancel{2}}}{\underset{3}{\cancel{15}}} = \frac{1}{12}$

The fractions we have added and subtracted so far have been very simple, but when common denominators are not so easily found a special treatment is required. We have to find the Lowest Common Multiple (L.C.M.). Here is a sum to work out.

$$\frac{5}{12} - \frac{8}{21}$$

How do we convert sheep (twelfths) and goats (twenty-firsts) into animals? Our first step has to be to find the L.C.M. of 12 and 21. We do this by breaking down 12 and 21 into Prime Factors (i.e. numbers which are divisible only by themselves and 1). The L.C.M. of 12 and 21 is arrived at thus:

Prime Factors

$$12 = 3 \times 2 \times 2$$
$$21 = 3 \qquad\quad \times 7$$

L.C.M. $= 3 \times 2 \times 2 \times 7 = 84$

This leaves us to proceed with the original calculation.

$$\frac{5}{12} = \frac{5 \times 7}{12 \times 7} = \frac{35}{84}$$

$$\frac{8}{21} = \frac{8 \times 4}{21 \times 4} = \frac{32}{84}$$

$$\frac{35}{84} - \frac{32}{84} = \frac{3}{84} = \frac{1}{28}$$

And here is another example where the calculation of an L.C.M. will be required.

$$\frac{5}{14} - \frac{4}{21}$$

The L.C.M. of 14 and 21?

Prime Factors

$$14 = 2 \times 7$$
$$21 = \quad 7 \times 3$$

$$\text{L.C.M.} = 2 \times 7 \times 3 = 42$$

$$\frac{5}{14} = \frac{5 \times 3}{14 \times 3} = \frac{15}{42}$$

$$\frac{4}{21} = \frac{4 \times 2}{21 \times 2} = \frac{8}{42}$$

$$\frac{15}{42} - \frac{8}{42} = \frac{7}{42} = \frac{1}{6}$$

We have dealt with multiplication, subtraction and addition of fractions and that leaves us to deal with division. One way of remembering what is required is to ask a simple question. How many quarters are there in a half? You can think of an orange again if you like. The answer is obviously 2. We know the answer and now we have to decide how to arrive at the required result.

$$\tfrac{1}{2} \div \tfrac{1}{4}$$

The first step is to invert (turn upside down) the divisor (the second fraction here). Then we change the dividing sign into a multiplication sign and work out the calculation.

$$\frac{1}{2} \times \frac{4}{1} = \frac{4}{2} = 2$$

Another example: $\frac{5}{8} \div \frac{3}{4} = \frac{5}{8} \times \frac{4}{3} = \frac{20}{24} = \frac{5}{6}$

A variation of the fraction is the ratio where a number is expressed in relation to another number. So, if there are 4 males and 9 females in a particular office the ratio of males to females will be expressed as 4 to 9 or 4 : 9. If 3 of the females in the office are married then the ratio of married to single women is 3 : 6 which will be reduced to, and expressed as, a ratio of 1 : 2.

Ratios are often used by accountants. One of the things they look for in a set of business accounts is the relationship between sales and stocks. From these figures they can calculate the Stock turn.

$$\text{Stock turn} = \frac{\text{Annual sales}}{\text{Average value of stocks}}$$

So if a furniture retailer sells £120000 of goods in a year, and carries an average of £20000 stock in his store, his Stock turn will be

$$\frac{£120000}{£20000} = 6$$

If the stock turns over 6 times in a year it means the stock is taking about 2 months to sell.

Suppose in the next accounts the figures change to £100000 for sales and £25000 for stock. This would show a Stock turn of

$$\frac{£100000}{£25000} = 4$$

This indicates that the stock turns over 4 times in the year, i.e. it takes about 3 months to sell stock. This is an obvious deterioration.

Here is a calculation for you to make. A newsagent carries a stock of £420 and his sales are £10080 in a year. What is his Stock turn?

How long does he expect to take to sell goods he has purchased? Why do you think he has such a high Stock turn compared to the furniture retailer?

Sometimes fractions are easy to convert into percentages and decimals, but the more difficult conversions are made thus:

$\frac{7}{32}$ as a percentage? Multiply by 100

$$\frac{7}{32} \times 100 = \frac{700}{32} = 21.875\%$$

and $\frac{7}{32}$ as a decimal? Divide 7 by 32

$32\overline{)\,7}$ = 0.21875 or 0.22 (to two decimal places).

If we have to cope with both fractions and decimals in a calculation, e.g.

$$\frac{3}{8} \times 1.25$$

we have to decide whether we want to answer in the form of a fraction or a decimal. First, let us look for a solution expressed as a fraction:

$$\frac{3}{8} \times 1\tfrac{1}{4} = \frac{3}{8} \times \frac{5}{4} = \frac{15}{32}$$

Next let us look for a solution expressed as a decimal

$$\frac{3}{8} \times 1.25 = \frac{3.75}{8} = 0.46875 \text{ or } 0.47 \text{ to two decimal places.}$$

Now consider some of the ways fractions might be used in business calculations. We might find, for example, that a store which specialises in the sale of denims marks down its prices in a sale by a third. That is a sizeable reduction and means that an article priced at £6 would be reduced by

$$\frac{1}{3} \times £6 = £2$$

So the reduced price would be £4.

A variation of this calculation would occur when we were asked to find the original price when only the sale price was known (because the price ticket had got lost?).

Suppose the sale price of a denim skirt in the same store was £11, what would the original price have been?

If two-thirds of original price $= £11$
then one-third ,, ,, ,, $= \frac{£11}{2}$

and the original price would have been

$$£\frac{11}{2} \times 3 = £\frac{33}{2} = £16.50$$

Another example: The Voltaires are a well-known pop group. They perform at a certain college's Rag Ball. They collect a cheque for £222.50 for the performance and this has to be divided between them in agreed proportions.

John, the lead singer, is entitled to ½
Tony, the lead guitarist, is entitled to $^3/_{10}$
and Gus, the drummer, is entitled to $^1/_5$
What do they each collect?

½ for John so divide £222.50 by 2	=	111.25
$^3/_{10}$ for Tony so 0.3 x £222.50	=	66.75
$^1/_5$ for Gus so divide £222.50 by 5	=	44.50
		£222.50

Another way of describing the division of receipts among the Voltaires would be to say they go to John, Tony and Gus in the ratios of 5 : 3 : 2, which, as we know, is the same as saying they receive 5/10ths, 3/10ths and 2/10ths respectively.

A less common calculation would occur when a person becomes bankrupt and is unable to pay his debts.

An example: Karl Kramer was a famous speedway star of the early 1970s. Then he was involved in a crash during the heats for the World Championship. He received spinal injuries which put an end to his speedway career. He still had expensive tastes, however, and his expenditure was much greater than his income. Eventually he was made bankrupt. He owed a total of £12537.50, and had assets (cash or things of value) totalling only £2507.50. If we put the assets over the debts (or liabilities) we see the fraction of the debts which can be paid.

$$\frac{£2507.50}{£12537.50} = \frac{1}{5}$$

Karl Kramer will be able to meet 1/5th of his debts; or, to put it in a conventional form, he will be able to pay 20p in the £. So if Kramer owed you £25 you could expect to receive 1/5th of £25, i.e. £5. You would expect to lose the other £20. This explains the care taken when goods are sold on credit.

DECIMALS

Decimal calculations are very common in business. They are the basis for all currency and metric calculations. Decimals are based on tenths:

0.3 is the same as 3/10ths
0.03 is the same as 3/100ths

When decimal fractions are added together, the decimal points should be placed under each other.

```
 1.225 +
 0.6
 3.15
 -----
 4.975
 -----
```

One can see with decimal calculations particularly how important it is to line up figures correctly. The same applies to subtractions.

```
  1.575
 -0.86
 ------
  0.715
 ------
```

For multiplication and division you should remember that you can multiply by 10 by moving the decimal point one place to the right. To multiply by 100 the decimal point is moved two places to the right. And so on.

By the same token we move decimal points one, two or three places to the left if we wish to divide by 10, 100 or 1000 respectively. Thus:

$$1.5 \times 10 = 15.0$$
$$4.065 \times 100 = 406.5$$
$$37.0 \div 10 = 3.7$$
$$26.25 \div 100 = .2625$$

The basic rule when multiplying decimals is to count the number of digits (figures) after the decimal point in both numbers being multiplied. The decimal point is then placed in the answer so that there are the same number of digits after the decimal point. The decimal points can be ignored while the multiplication proceeds. For example:

4.35 x 1.5 (note there are three digits after the decimal points)

```
 435 x
  15
----
4350
2175
----
6525
----
```

Answer = 6.525 (note the three digits after the decimal points).

For division, first convert the divisor into units, i.e. single numbers, by moving the decimal point to the left or right as required. Then move the decimal point the same number of places in the same direction in the number being divided. Finally, work out the division, paying careful attention to the position of both the digits and the decimal points. Thus:

$3.75 \div .25 = 37.5 \div 2.5$ (decimal point moved one place to the right in each case)

```
       15.0
      -----
2.5 ) 37.5
      25
      ---
      125
      125
      ---
      ...          Answer = 15.0
```

One can make a rough check by doing the division without reference to the decimal elements.

$37 \div 2 = 18.5$, which indicates that the decimal point is in the correct position. 15.0 is closer to 18.5 than the alternatives of 1.85 or 185.0.

Another example:

$72.3 \div 56.5 = 7.23 \div 5.65$

```
       1.3
      -----
5.65) 7.345
      5.65
      -----
      1.695
      1.695
      -----
      ....         Answer = 1.3
```

Rough check $7 \div 5 = 1.4$, so answer is of correct order.

You should be familiar with decimals, especially since they are now used to express prices. For example, you see a T-shirt in a shop with a price tag of £3.99 on it. Thus you know then that it costs 1p – or 1/100th of a £ – less than £4.

With currencies throughout the world it is usual to find the main unit divided into 100 parts. Thus:

100 cents = $1 (U.S.A. and Canada) 100 pfennigs = 1 mark (W. Germany)
100 centimes = 1 franc (France) 100 centimos = 1 peseta (Spain)

So if Wayne is on holiday in New York and decides to treat himself to a double-decker hamburger he might have to pay $1.50 for the pleasure. With an exchange rate of $2 to the £, the equivalent price in Britain would be 75p.

$2 = £1, so $1 = £0.50 and $1.50 = £0.75, or 75p

Weights are also calculated decimally. The most common weights used in Europe are grams and kilograms. There are 1000 grams in a kilogram. If you want a comparison between these weights and the lb and oz with which we are familiar in Britain:

1 kilo(gram) = 2.2 lb
1 oz = 28⅓ grams (or 30 grams if you want an approximation)

So if Jennifer is on holiday in Germany and sees some Golden Delicious apples for sale at 2.80 marks per kilo(gram), should she be tempted? If there are 4 marks to the £, what would the apples cost per lb in British money?

If 4 marks = £1 then 1 mark = 25p
and so 2.80 marks = 2.80 x 25p = 70p
If 2.2 lb (1 kilo) cost 70p
1 lb would cost $\frac{70}{2.2}$p
i.e. 32p per lb (to nearest penny)

The main metric measurements relating to distance are centimetres, metres and kilometres.

100 cm = 1 m   1000 m = 1 km

Comparing the old measurements with the new, one metre is approximately one yard – or more precisely 39 inches, and one mile is approximately 1.6 kilometres or 1.609 kilometres (accurate to three decimal places).

Suppose Carol is going to Scotland for her holidays. One of her friends at college offers to take her to Edinburgh and pick her up on the way back so long as Carol shares the cost of the petrol for her part of the journey. It will be a journey of 230 kilometres each way, and the petrol consumption will be approximately 25 kilometres to the gallon. If the price of petrol were 85p to the gallon, how much would Carol have to pay for the trip?

The journey is 460 km (230 km x 2)

$\frac{460}{25}$ = number of gallons expected to be consumed

$\frac{460}{25} \times £0.85$ = cost of journey

When shared between two, Carol will have to pay £7.82. No doubt she would give her friend £8.

(If you have a pocket calculator you might check this answer.)

Next let us suppose that the price of the petrol varies according to whether it is bought from a Contex or a Voiture petrol station. Contex offer petrol at 85p per gallon as above, but Voiture are offering their petrol at 24p per litre. Which petrol is more economic (assuming the grade is identical)? How much would Carol save if the cheaper petrol were purchased? (1 gallon = 4.546 litres to three decimal places.)

If $\frac{460}{25}$ = consumption in gallons

then $\frac{460}{25} \times 4.546$ = consumption in litres

and $\frac{460}{25} \times 4.546 \times £0.24$ = cost of Voiture petrol

The cost of Voiture petrol would amount to £20.08, half of which would be £10.04, compared to £7.82 – an extra cost of £2.22. (Again, you might check the answer with your pocket calculator.)

PERCENTAGES

The relation between fractions, decimals and percentages can be seen from Figure 1.1. Note particularly the correspondence of the digits in the second and third columns.

Percent	Fraction	Decimal
0%	0	0.00
5%	1/20	0.05
10%	1/10	0.1
15%	3/20	0.15
20%	1/5	0.2
25%	1/4	0.25
30%	3/10	0.3
35%	7/20	0.35
40%	2/5	0.4
45%	9/20	0.45
50%	1/2	0.5
55%	11/20	0.55
60%	3/5	0.6
65%	13/20	0.65
70%	7/10	0.7
75%	3/4	0.75
80%	4/5	0.8
85%	17/20	0.85
90%	9/10	0.9
95%	19/20	0.95
100%	1	1.00

FIGURE 1.1

One of the most common calculations in business relates to percentages. When you buy goods from the shops you will find the shopkeeper having to add V.A.T. to the cost of the purchase. This is a tax which is eventually paid over to the Government.

'And then we have to add 8% V.A.T.,' says the shopkeeper, and if you have no idea how to work out 8% of anything, you either have to trust his calculation, or someone else's calculation!

Perhaps you will find yourself selling goods in your job. Your employer offers you commission on sales to encourage you to make a big effort. You work hard. You have already decided how you are going to spend your bonus for the month.

'Let me see,' says the Wages Clerk, 'you get 7½% commission on sales don't you. You've sold £832 worth of goods this month. 7½% on £832. That's £37.50 commission.'

Do you say, 'Thank you' politely, or 'I think you've made a mistake'?

You might find yourself involved with percentages at the most unlikely times. You could be on a Saturday morning shopping spree. You come to the store which sells records. 'Bargain Week,' it says on the window, '15% off all marked prices.' You find an L.P. featuring your favourite group. £5.25 is the price according to the label.

'£5.25 less 15%,' says the assistant, pulling out a pocket calculator, 'Where would we be without these things?'

The calculator shows the discount to be 34p, so the assistant charges you £4.91. Have you been charged correctly? She used a calculator, so it must be right? Or could she have pressed a wrong button?

Or you may be getting on well with your job as sales assistant and your employer wants to give you more responsible work, working out the 'mark-up' on merchandise, i.e. the amount he adds to the cost of the articles for his gross profit.

'Mark-up is 12½%,' he explains.

And you look at him vacantly.

Hardly the way to achieve early promotion!

Perhaps it is apparent why we need to be able to make calculations such as these – in life generally – and in business particularly. The alternative is to be at the mercy of other people – or to be a slave to the calculating-machines rather than their masters.

How do we calculate a percentage?

6% means 6 for every 100, so 6% on £100 is £6 and 6% on £200 is twice as much i.e. £12.

What are the mechanics of the calculations? Here are two methods to think about.

Method One

6% of £100?

$$\frac{6}{100} \times £100$$

$$= \frac{6}{1\not{0}\not{0}} \times £1\not{0}\not{0}$$

$$= £6$$

6% of £200?

$$\frac{6}{100} \times £200$$

$$= \frac{6}{1\not{0}\not{0}} \times £2\not{0}\not{0}$$

$$= £12$$

Method Two

6% of £100?
6% x £100 = 6 x £1.00 (moving the decimal point two places to the left)
= £6.00

6% of £200?
6% x £200 = 6 x £2.00
= £12.00

Some simple calculations for practice

5% of £100 = £5	5% of £150 = ?
5% of £200 = £10	5% of £250 = ?
5% of £300 = £15	5% of £500 = ?
10% of £300 = £30	10% of £450 = ?

Percentages as fractions

10% is the same as one-tenth (1/10)
20% is the same as one-fifth (1/5)
(there are five 20%s in 100%)
25% is the same as one-quarter (1/4)

Examples

(1) 10% of £565?
10% = 1/10 1/10th of £565 (found by moving decimal point one place to the left) = £56.5

(2) 12½% of £62.40?
12½% = 1/8 1/8th of £62.40 = 8) 62.40
Answer = £7.80

(3) 2½% of £35.20?
2½% = 1/40 1/40th of £35.20 = 40) 35.20
4) 3.520
Answer = £0.88 or 88p

(4) 5% of £1.75?
5% = 1/20 1/20th of £1.75 = 20) 1.75
= 2) 0.175
= £.0875
Answer = 9p to nearest penny

(5) 16 2/3% of £162?
16 2/3% = 1/6 1/6th of £162 = 6) 162
Answer = £27

Some less common percentages

How can one calculate 1¾% on £60? Again there are two methods.

Method One

If 1% on £60 = 60p (moving the decimal point two places to the left)
½% on £60 = 30p (divide the previous result by 2)
and ¼% on £60 = 15p (divide previous result by 2)
1¾% on £60 = £1.05 (add all previous results)

Method Two

$$1\tfrac{3}{4} = 7/4 \qquad \frac{7}{400} \times £60 = \frac{7}{40\not{0}} \times £6\not{0} = \frac{7}{\not{4}\not{0}_{20}} \times \not{6}^{3}$$

$$£\,\frac{21}{20} = £1.05$$

Choice of Method

The first method is particularly simple, but it assumes that the percentage can be broken down conveniently. When this is not possible, the second method is likely to be preferable.

Some examples

(1) 1⅝% of £3165.50?
If 1% = £31.655
4/8% = 15.8275
1/8% = 3.9568
1⅝% = £51.4393

(2) 6½% of £75?
If 1% = £0.75
5% = 3.75
½% = 0.375
6½% = £4.875

(3) 8¾% of £260? (the second method is probably more appropriate for this calculation)

8¾% = 35/4

$$\frac{35}{400} \times £260 = \frac{35}{40\not{0}} \times 26\not{0} = \frac{\not{3}\not{5}^{7}}{\not{4}\not{0}_{8}} \times 26 = \frac{7}{\not{8}_{4}} \times \not{2}\not{6}^{13} = \frac{91}{4}$$

$$= £22.75$$

Simple interest

One of the commonest percentage calculations in business involves the so-called 'simple' interest. It works like this:

If you deposit money with a Building Society, it will give you interest on your investment. The interest rate will be expressed as, say, 7% per annum. This means that for every year you keep £100 in the society you will receive £7 interest. Of course, £50 will entitle you to £3.50 interest, and £25 will entitle you to £1.75 interest.

Apart from performing the normal percentage calculation you will also need to multiply this by the number of years for which the investment is made in order to work out the total interest payments over the period.

For example, suppose you invest £200 in a Building Society for 3 years at an interest rate of 7% per annum. What is the total amount of interest you may withdraw during the period?

$$£200 \times \frac{7}{100} \times 3 = £2\not{0}\not{0} \times \frac{7}{100} \times 3 = £42$$

Or again, suppose you deposit £300 for 4 years at 5½%. What will the total interest payments be?

$$£300 \times \frac{11}{200} \times 4 = £3\not{0}\not{0} \times \frac{11}{\underset{1}{\not{2}\not{0}\not{0}}} \times \overset{2}{\not{4}} = £66$$

And, slightly more complicated, suppose you deposit £350 for 2½ years at 6½%. What would the simple interest be? The calculation would start

$$£350 \times \frac{13}{200} \times \frac{5}{2} \qquad \text{Can you finish it?}$$

If you do not withdraw the interest from the account, then the interest is added to the capital sum invested. Going back to the first example, the capital for the second year becomes £107 and the next year's interest is calculated on this sum. This is what is called "compound" interest – as opposed to the 'simple' interest we have been dealing with here.

Calculating the whole from a given percentage

Suppose Judy Maguire, a well-known pop star, is looking for a new outfit for a television appearance. She finds a rather colourful outfit in a Carnaby Street boutique. The price is £93.60 and the saleslady tells her that this was 75% of the original price. If that were so, what would the original price have been?

The calculation can be made in the following way:

If 75% of the original price = £93.60

1% would be $\frac{£93.60}{75}$

and 100% would be $\frac{£93.60 \times 100}{75}$

$$\frac{£93.60 \times \overset{4}{\cancel{100}}}{\underset{3}{\cancel{75}}} = 31.20 \times 4 = £124.80$$

Judy recently cut a disc for a well-known recording company. At the end of six months the recording company send her a cheque for £642 as royalties. If the royalties were calculated at 6% on net sales, what were the net sales?

If 6% of net sales = £642

1% would be $\frac{£642}{6}$

and 100% would be $\frac{£642}{6} \times 100$

$$6\,)\,\underline{64200}$$
$$\underline{10700}$$

Answer = £10,700

Expressing one quantity as a percentage of another

Judy's agent is concerned to find out what sort of people are her fans. Do they tend to be young or old? Male or female? The agent got the following information from the audiences at The Tivoli Bar, Manchester, where she was starring last week.

Analysis of audience by age and sex

	under 21	21–50	over 50
Male	1222	114	7
Female	764	37	29

What percentage of her audience were male and under 21?

$$\frac{\text{Males under 21} = 1222}{\text{Total audience} = 2173}$$

Percentage of males under the age of 21 = (1222/2173) x 100
(Note that when you want to express a proportion as a percentage you multiply the proportion by 100.)

```
          56.23
2173 )122200
      10865
       13550
       13038
         5120
         4346
          7740
          6519
          ----
          1221
```

Answer = 56.2% (We can take this to one decimal place. Any greater degree of accuracy would be spurious.)

What percentage of the audience were female?

$$\text{Total females} = \frac{830}{2173} \times 100$$

Work this calculation for yourself and check your answer with a pocket calculator, if you have one.

Calculating percentage change

Judy has recently completed a rather startling autobiography entitled *Night Freight from Tiger Bay*. Thanks to some useful television publicity the number of books sold over the first three months since publication have been quite high.

	(1) Actual sales	(2) Sales rounded to nearest hundred
July	4186	4200
August	5079	5100
September	3257	3300

Notice first the value of rounding figures – in this case to the nearest 100 books. It is much easier to compare the sales over the three months when unnecessary detail has been eliminated. This is the purpose of rounding the figures.

Using the rounded figures we can then ask: What percentage increase in sales was there between July and August?

Sales increased by 900.
Sales were previously 4200.

$$\frac{900}{4200} \times 100 = \frac{900}{42\not{0}\not{0}} \times 1\not{0}\not{0} = \frac{\overset{150}{\not{9}\not{0}\not{0}}}{\underset{7}{\not{4}\not{2}}}$$

$$= \underline{21.4\%}$$

The answer is given accurately to one decimal place, though one is bound to lose accuracy to some extent by rounding figures. If a high degree of accuracy was called for it would be unwise to round the figures.

We can ask finally, what percentage decrease was there in sales between August and September?

Sales fell by 1800
Sales fell from 5100

$$\frac{1800}{5100} \times 100 = \frac{18\not{0}\not{0}}{51\not{0}\not{0}} \times 100$$

```
     35.2
51 ) 1800  (
     153
      270
      255
       150
       102
        48
```

Another way of making figures easier to read is to produce an answer to, say, two significant figures. In the case in question this would mean taking only the first two figures in the answer, i.e. 35%. In the circumstances little is lost by saying that sales fell by 35% rather than 35.2%.

The loss of accuracy in both rounding numbers and working to two significant figures might be tested here by using column 1 instead of column 2 for the calculations, and then seeing how far away from an increase of 21% and a decrease of 35% are your refined answers.

AVERAGES

It is not difficult to register a single figure in the mind, but a range of figures can be confusing. We cannot easily absorb the details meaningfully until we simplify the mass of figures by calculating the average. Here is a real-life example.

Susan was looking for a post as an audio typist. She was offered a post which paid £28.50 per week, but she had four friends already at work and she found they were drawing £26.75, £28.75, £30, and £27.50 per week respectively. Should she take the post she had been offered?

Susan found the average pay packet of her friends by totalling their pay and dividing the total by the number of friends. Thus

```
       £26.75
        28.75
        30.00
        27.50
       ------
4 )    113.00
       ------
       £28.25  = average pay in the group.*
       ======
```

---

*In order to avoid confusion between this type of average and other averages such as the *median* and the *mode,* mathemeticians usually refer to this as the arithmetic mean.

As the pay being offered to Susan was above the average being earned by her friends, she was encouraged to accept the job.

Another measure we can take in a range of figures is the so-called *median.* The median is the middle figure in a given range. Take the ages of the girls in the office where Susan is about to start work.

	yrs	mths		yrs	mths		yrs	mths
Sarah	18	10	Gail	22	11	Sandra	19	9
Jane	17	5	Angela	16	10	Liz	24	2
Alison	19	7	Penny	16	11	Abigail	16	10

What can you say about the ages of these girls? You can certainly find out their average age. The ages total 173 years and 3 months. There are 9 girls, so their average age is 19 years and 3 months. But you can also place their ages in descending order and this gives you the following series.

24.2; 22.11; 19.9; 19.7; 18.10; 17.5; 16.11; 16.10; 16.10.

Which is the middle figure? We find it by adding 1 to the number of girls in the group – and dividing the total by 2, i.e.

$$\frac{9+1}{2} = \frac{10}{2} = \text{5th figure in the series.}$$

Thus the median girl/age is Sarah/18 yrs 10 mths.

Another measure used occasionally is the *mode*. If we look at the same group of girls, this time showing their O-level passes, we find the following situation.

O-level passes

Sarah	1	Gail	1	Sandra	1
Jane	0	Angela	2	Liz	2
Alison	2	Penny	2	Abigail	0

The mode is the most frequent figure appearing in a series, so 2 O-levels is the mode here.

When you calculate the average (arithmetic mean), the median and the mode for a range of figures you have performed some useful research on the composition of the group.

VISUAL PRESENTATION

It is sometimes possible to present statistics visually – in the form of graphs or diagrams – so as to make their meaning clear at a glance. Figures need to be studied and interpreted, but a diagram might convey facts at a glance. Consider the case of Intrigue Cosmetics Inc., an American firm selling a variety of beauty products in Britain. The statistics below indicate the value of their sales during the past two years. They also show the sales of their competitors. Intrigue Cosmetics are not only concerned with their sales figures. They are also concerned with their share of the market.

	Sales in £000	
	This year	Last year
Intrigue Cosmetics	6804	6325
Other manufacturers	40811	25426
Total	47615	31751

Do the executives at Intrigue Cosmetics congratulate themselves for achieving an increase in sales (incidentally, what percentage is the increase?), or can they expect to be criticised for a disappointing performance?

The diagrams below in Figure 1.2 are called *pie charts* and when you look at them you will see why Intrigue Cosmetics have not done very well over the past year – and that such diagrams can be very useful.

If you have to draw a pie chart from data given it is necessary first to recall that there are 360° (degrees) in a full circle. Then we take the total which is to be sliced up (or apportioned) and relate this to the 360°. Thus:

$$\text{If £31751 (last year's total)} = 360^0$$

$$\text{£1} = \frac{360^0}{31751}$$

$$\text{and £6325 (Intrigue's share)} = \frac{360^0}{31751} \times 6325^0$$

$$= 72^0 \text{ to nearest degree}$$

Using a protractor we can then allocate 72^0 of the 360^0 to indicate Intrigue's share of the total last year.

We could assume from this that the other manufacturers would take

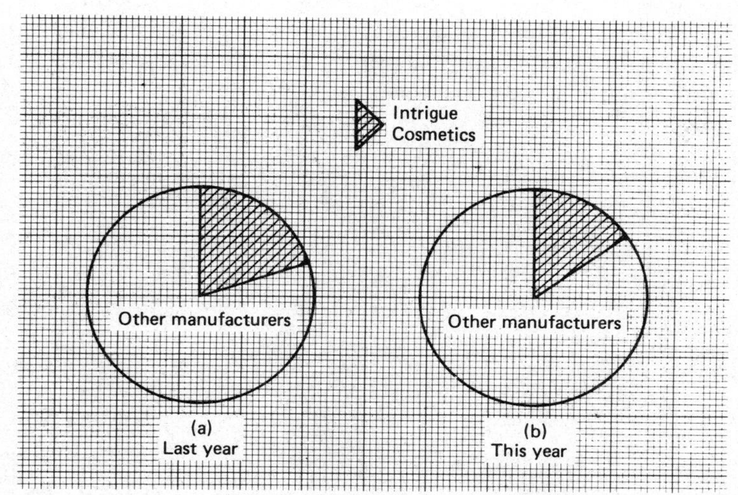

FIGURE 1.2 *Sales of Intrigue Cosmetics as compared to total sales of cosmetics*

up the remaining 288^0 of the pie, but by working out the other manufacturers' shares independently we are also checking our first calculation, which we would want to do anyway. So

$$\text{If} \quad £1 = \frac{360^0}{31751}$$

then other manufacturer's share

$$= \frac{360^0}{31751} \times 25426^0$$

$= 288^0$ to nearest degree

$288^0 + 72^0 = 360^0$ (check)

These calculations are quite formidable and one can see the value of a pocket calculator especially where, as here, the second calculation can be used as a check on the first.

If we bear in mind the similarity between the basic principles of the pocket calculator and the electronic computer, we can understand why the latter are so highly prized in business. More complex problems call for more complex equipment.

Another form of visual presentation is the *bar chart*. Those shown in Figure 1.3 refer to attendances at Regent Group cinemas in the London area. The cinema proprietors are checking on changes in the popularity of the different types of film they show in their 37 cinemas. The company took over this chain of cinemas three years ago, and the attendances relate to these first three years of operation.

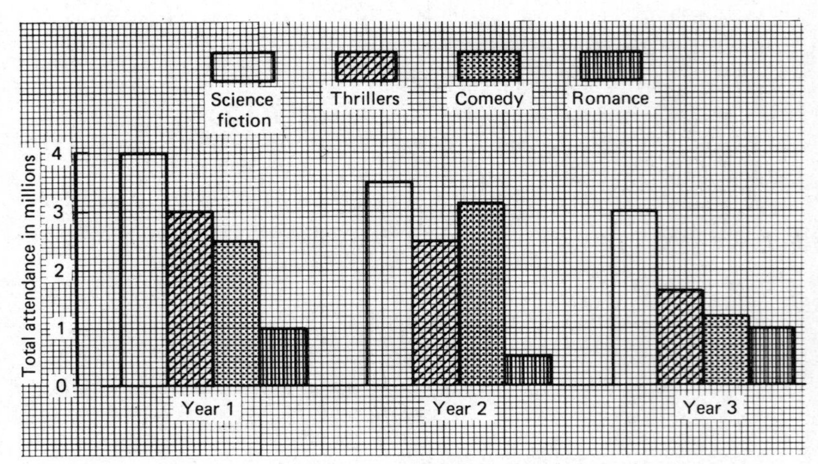

FIGURE 1.3 *Cinema attendance*

What conclusions can you draw from simply studying these diagrams?

Perhaps the most common form of visual presentation used in business is the *graph*. The principal point to note about graphs is that they are two-dimensional. The x-axis records one dimension – this is often, but not necessarily, the time dimension. The y-axis records another range of data which is somehow related to the first.

Suppose that Susan spends most of her spare time at discotheques. The table below shows how many visits she has made to discos over the last six months.

	Mar	Apr	May	June	July	Aug
Visits	17	20	12	15	10	7

This information can be plotted on a graph in the manner shown in Figure 1.4.

Apart from indicating past information the graph can help you to anticipate future events. For example, how often do you think Susan will visit discos in September? 14 times? 20 times? 4 times? Which of these is most likely on the evidence here?

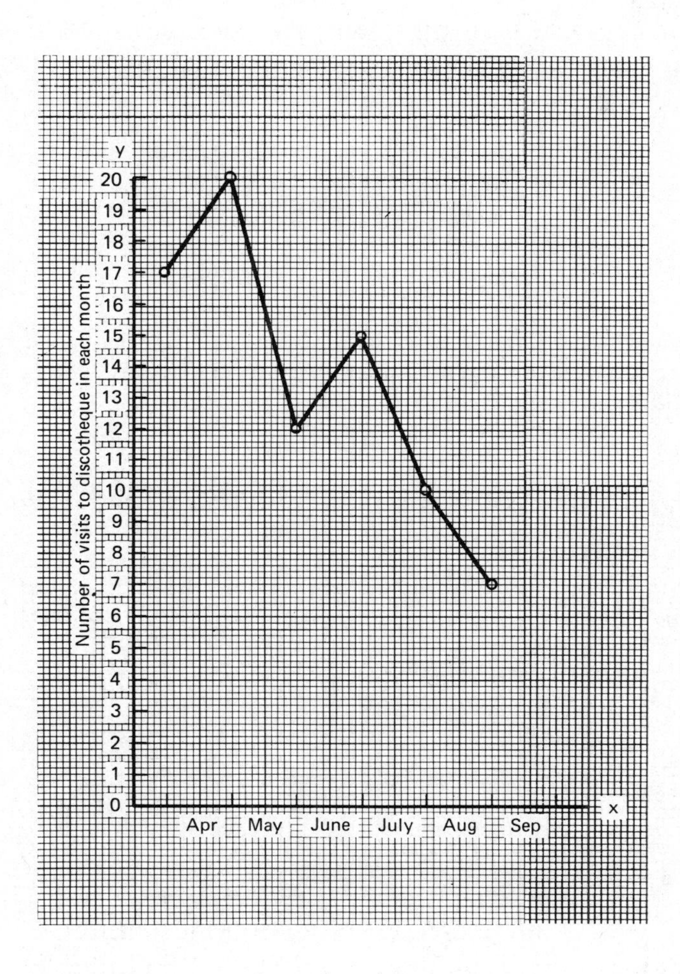

FIGURE 1.4 *Visits to discotheques during last six months*

Is there a danger in making such assumptions? Susan's attendance at discos fell off from May to August, but it may have been because of the fine weather, or because she had taken up cycling. She might have a new boyfriend who takes her Tenpin Bowling. In the autumn and winter she may go back to the discos with renewed enthusiasm. So it is obviously dangerous to project trends on this sort of data.

An example of a graph with a better predictive value would be one showing increases in the cost of living over a period of time.

	*Cost of living**
January	£17.00
February	£17.20
March	£17.30
April	£17.50
May	£17.80

* As represented by the purchase of a similar basket of food sufficient to feed a family of four (average weekly cost during the month).

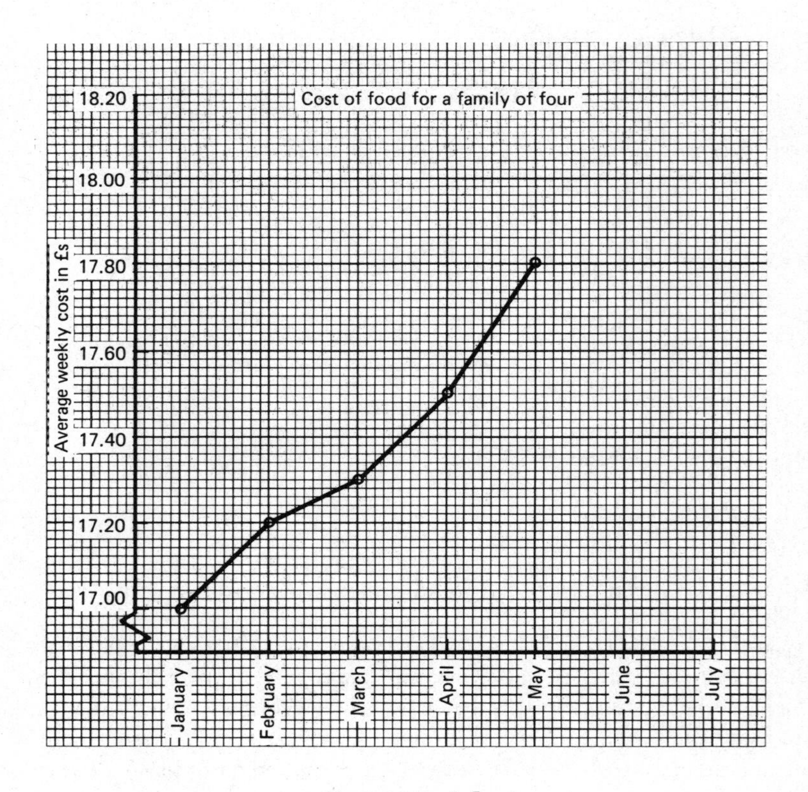

FIGURE 1.5

One could predict the likely rise in the cost of food for succeeding months with a fair degree of accuracy.

You will note that in Figure 1.5 there is a broken line at the base of the Y axis. This is to show we are not starting from zero. The lower values have been excluded. This enables us to indicate the changes which have occurred on a larger scale.

Graphs such as this are used to chart sales, wages, unemployment and an infinite variety of business data.

2 The Assignments

In this, the main section of the book, you will find a series of short assignments. A real-life situation will be presented to you and you will be expected to work through the exercise as directed. Your tutor may require you to work on your own for the first part of the assignment, or he may work through the exercise with the whole group. But at some stage of each assignment you will be expected to discuss problems with your class-mates – under the general guidance of your tutor.

You will find you are given a lot more background information here than is usual in mathematical exercises, and this is an attempt to make the work both more realistic and more interesting.

The oral work is aimed at familiarising you with the sort of discussions which are likely to take place in a real-life working situation. At work you will be expected to exchange ideas and work co-operatively with the rest of the staff. In the circumstances it is probably wise to learn now (i) how to make points acceptably, (ii) how to listen patiently while other people express their opinions, and (iii) how to offer criticisms constructively and politely.

The assignments are also designed to make you *think* arithmetically and mathematically. This is something more than 'doing sums' mechanically, though elsewhere – in Sections 3 and 4 specifically – you will have the opportunity to develop these essential mechanical skills.

The assignments should also help you to understand how calculations are a normal part of life generally, as well as being a vital ingredient in business.

It is suggested that work on the Assignments should be integrated with the Speed and Accuracy Exercises in Section 3 as far as possible. The learning process is designed to continue through both sections.

Note: Where you are asked to complete a bill or invoice in the Assignments, do not just put the figures on a scrap of paper – which is easily lost – but copy out the whole bill (etc.) in your work book. This will give you practice in setting out data in a clear and orderly way, and the work will be available for checking if the answer proves to be wrong!

1 FESTIVAL OF FLOWERS

Marion Cavendish owns a florist's shop in Melton Mowbray and it is called the Festival of Flowers. Much of her sales are to people passing by – so-called 'passing trade' – but she also has a number of customers who have monthly accounts. In particular there are a few large hotels which buy flowers to place in their reception areas.

Marion's assistant, Alison, fills in the details on the monthly statements, but Marion works out the amounts to go in the cash column. She does this since her assistant, who is rather dependent on her pocket calculator, charged Lady Strachey's account with £17.56 for two dozen yellow chrysanthemums at £1.25 per dozen. Lady Strachey is one of Marion's best customers and she was understandably annoyed by the error.

Below you see the monthly statements which were sent out for last March. You are asked to complete these statements in the same way that Marion did. All prices include V.A.T. (value-added-tax).

It is interesting to note that, since decimalisation, florists buy their stock in tens within the trade. But many, like Marion Cavendish, continue to sell them in dozens because this is what their customers prefer.

Statement (for March)
Montmarcie Hotel, Wollaton

			(£)
1	March	3 doz Spring Roses at £2.12 per doz	
14	,,	6 doz King Alfred Daffodils at 60p per doz	
25	,,	5 assorted Ferns at £1.85 each	
28	,,	6 doz Mixed Daffodils at 65p per doz	
			———
			———

Statement (for March)
Station Hotel, Bolchester

		(£)
5 March	2 doz Spring Roses at £2.12 per doz	
13 ,,	7 doz King Alfred Daffodils at 60p per doz	
19 ,,	1 gross White Harvest Narcissus at 75p per doz	
25 ,,	3 doz Mixed Iris at £1.35 per doz	
		____
		____

Statement (for March)
Lady Cynthia Strachey, Allbury Manor

		(£)
1 March	18 Spring Roses at £2.12 per doz	
15 ,,	4 doz King Alfred Daffodils at 60p per doz	
	6 Tiger Orchids at £1.95 each	
28 ,,	7 assorted Ferns at £1.85 each	
		____
	less 10% discount	____
		____

Statement (for March)
Mr Grantham Rogers, Witherley

		(£)
1 March	Brought forward from February	6.85
5 ,,	6 doz Spring Roses at £2.12 per doz	
25 ,,	6 doz Mixed Iris at £1.35 per doz	
	6 assorted Ferns at £1.85 each	
28 ,,	7 potted Aubrietia at 38p each	
		____
		____

Statement (for March)
The Falcon Hotel, Allbury

		(£)
1 March	5 doz Spring Roses at £2.12 per doz	
14 ,,	7 doz King Alfred Daffodils at 60p per doz	
21 ,,	½ gross White Harvest Narcissus at 75p per doz	
25 ,,	4 doz Mixed Iris at £1.25 per doz	
		____
		____

Questions for the group to discuss

1 Do you think Marion is wise to let these customers have plants and flowers before they pay for them? Why do you think she gives her customers credit? What would she do if they did not pay promptly?
2 How do you think the pocket calculator could be used successfully to ensure that mistakes are not made at the Festival of Flowers?
3 Has the group spotted an apparent mistake that Alison made when drafting the statements?
4 Only Lady Strachey is given a discount. What justification might there be for this?
5 What is value-added-tax?

2 BOATING HOLIDAYS

Rivercraft Holidays Ltd have four craft which they offer on hire to holiday-makers. The hirers are able to take the craft away from the base – on the upper reaches of the *Thames* – and, within certain limits, they can journey at will in the luxury motor launches. The hiring charges are set out below and include the cost of a starting 10 gallons of diesel fuel:

Hire charges per craft per week, including V.A.T. (£)

	Bahama	*Viking*	*Heron*	*Dolphin*
Before end of April	128	148	153	165
During May and June	138	159	165	177
During July	156	178	185	197
During August	179	206	212	224
After August	130	160	168	180
Number of persons allowed on the craft	3	4	5	6

The hiring charge is calculated according to the period in which the commencement of the hire falls. Thus a week's holiday starting on 28 July for the *Bahama* would be £156. But if a second week was required, from 4 August, the charge for the second week would be £179.

Your first task

Complete the booking forms below by showing the amounts involved at (a) (b) and (c) in each case. Then calculate the total of the deposits required from the hirers – and the total amount remaining due.

Booking form

Name of craft	*Heron*
Commencing date of hire	18 June
Period of hire	1 week
Name of hirer	Mark Gibbons
Hiring charge	£ . . . .(a)
15% deposit required	£ . . . .(b)
Amount outstanding	£ . . . .(c)

Booking form

Name of craft	*Bahama*
Commencing date of hire	29 April
Period of hire	2 weeks
Name of hirer	Karl Sachs
Hiring charge	£ . . . .(a)
15% deposit required	£ . . . .(b)
Amount outstanding	£ . . . .(c)

Booking form

Name of craft	*Dolphin*
Commencing date of hire	18 August
Period of hire	2 weeks
Name of hirer	Mrs Mildred Prentice
Hiring charge	£ . . . .(a)
15% deposit required	£ . . . .(b)
Amount outstanding	£ . . . .(c)

Booking form

Name of craft	*Viking*
Commencing date of hire	20 August
Period of hire	3 weeks
Name of hirer	Tony Adamson
Hiring charge	£ . . . .(a)
15% deposit required	£ . . . .(b)
Amount outstanding	£ . . . .(c)

Booking form

Name of craft	*Heron*
Commencing date of hire	2 September
Period of hire	2 weeks
Name of hirer	Graham Stiles
Hiring charge	£........................(a)
15% deposit required	£........................(b)
Amount outstanding	£........................(c)

Your second task

Working in groups of twos and threes you are asked to complete the following table so as to show the average cost per person for each of the craft throughout the season. The first figure in each row has been worked out for you.

Charges per person per week (including V.A.T.)

	Bahama	*Viking*	*Heron*	*Dolphin*
Before end of April	£42.67	£37.00	£30.60	£27.50
During May and June				
During July				
During August				
After August				

What do you notice about these charges? How would you justify the differences?

Your third task

There would obviously be complaints if there were any double bookings of craft by Rivercraft Holidays Ltd. Discuss together ways in which double bookings might be avoided. Try to produce a detailed plan to overcome the problem. If you decide to use some sort of chart to plot bookings, what would it look like?

3 SUNNYBROOK FARM

This is a small farm on the outskirts of Bristol. George Pettigrew and his family farm the 550 acres, almost the whole of which is given over to dairy farming. His herd of Guernsey cows has won a number of prizes for him at dairy shows over the years. Most of the milk yield goes to the Milk Marketing Board for distribution, but George continues to run a milk round which his father started 50 years ago. There are only four roundsmen and they sell home-baked bread (Samantha Pettigrew's speciality), free-range eggs (one size only – very large) and, of course the specially creamy milk.

The Pettigrew's daughter, Tina, has two functions on the farm. She has to feed the chickens and collect the eggs, and she also has to look after the clerical side of the milk round. At the end of each day the roundsmen bring in a *sales and returns list* and Tina has to calculate how much is due to be handed in. She also has to calculate the bonus the roundsmen have earned. They are entitled to a 5% bonus on top of their normal wages and this is calculated on the total of their daily sales.

You see below the forms that Tina has to complete when the roundsmen return at the end of the day. Working together in groups of twos and threes see if you can complete the forms for her. She has already completed the first one, but you should check it to make sure her arithmetic is correct.

Sales and returns list – Derek Chalk

	Out	*Returned*	*Sales*	*Cash*
Milk (pints)	500	32	468	£46.80
Bread (loaves)	60	2	58	14.50
Eggs	240	108	132	6.60
				£67.90

Commission at 5% = £3.35

Sales and returns list – Ken Dale

	Out	*Returned*	*Sales*	*Cash*
Milk (pints)	364	15		
Bread (loaves)	36	3		
Eggs	120	36		

Commission at 5% =

Sales and returns list – Bob Barratt

	Out	*Returned*	*Sales*	*Cash*
Milk (pints)	440	28		
Bread (loaves)	48	12		
Eggs	120	17		

Commission at 5% =

Sales and returns list – Jeff Agar

	Out	*Returned*	*Sales*	*Cash*
Milk (pints)	600	107		
Bread (loaves)	78	28		
Eggs	36	0		

Commission at 5% =

Questions for the group

1 Do you think it is a good idea to pay the roundsmen in this way, with a flat sum of, say, £35 a week plus a bonus on all sales? Can you think of other ways they might be paid?
2 Jeff Agar is new to the job. Looking at his sales and returns list what advice do you think Tina might give him? (Note that the roundsmen decide for themselves how much milk, etc. they should take on their rounds.)
3 Why do you think the Pettigrew's milk round will probably go out of business eventually? What advantages do the big firms have?

(*Note*: The price of the milk and other products has not been mentioned specifically, but of course you can work this out by referring to the items sold and the cash received on Derek Chalk's List.)

4 THE BELVEDERE HOTEL

The Belvedere is one of the smaller private hotels in Brighton and Sarah Travers is the receptionist there. If there is one thing that pleases her about her job it is that she does not have to do any maths. Maths was always her worst subject at school. But one day the proprietress, Mrs Agostini, had to visit a sick relative. It was a Saturday and Mrs Agostini had just enough time to make out details on the bills of the people who were leaving the hotel on that day, but she was not able to complete the bills. She had to leave that to be done by Sarah.

Here are the bills in question and after them comes the *tariff* indicating the prices that Sarah had to charge:

The Belvedere Hotel, Brighton

Mr & Mrs Palmer – Room 18

14 nights stay
6 lunches
14 early morning teas
14 early morning coffees

add 8% V.A.T.

The Belvedere Hotel, Brighton

Mr J. Fisher – Room 2

7 nights stay
7 lunches
7 early morning teas

add 8% V.A.T.

The Belvedere Hotel, Brighton

Mr & Mrs James Cramton – Room 21

3 nights stay
6 early morning teas

add 8% V.A.T.

The Belvedere Hotel, Brighton

Miss Margaret Pritchard – Room 1

5 nights stay
5 lunches
5 early morning coffees

add 8% V.A.T.

The Belvedere Hotel, Brighton

Mrs Michelle Richardson – Room 7

21 nights stay
6 lunches
3 early morning teas

add 8% V.A.T.

Tariff

Per night – including evening meal and breakfast

£6.00 per night single (rooms 1–9)
£10.00 per night double (rooms 10–22)

Lunches (extra) £1.35 per meal
Early morning teas 18p each; coffee 27p each

Your task

Pretend you are Sarah and complete the bills she would have had to present to the guests before they left the hotel. How much should she collect from the five guests in all? What was the total V.A.T. payable on the five bills?

A further task for the group to consider together

We can see here how Mrs Agostini makes her living out of the Belvedere Hotel, but can you draw up a list of payments that she might have to pay out during the course of a typical year? Are you sure you have not left any important items off the list?

5 THE BOOKSELLERS

Julian Thornhill had always liked books. He read books as often as he could and, although he was not a great scholar, it came as no surprise to his parents when he decided to join a small publishing firm. He started off working in the Order and Dispatch Department and his job was to deal with the invoices which were sent to various firms throughout the country. He had to look at the catalogue prices of the books and then complete the details on the invoices which had been partially made out.

You can see here the *Catalogue* from which Julian took the prices of the various books and below that is a selection of the invoices he was required to complete:

Catalogue

Title	*Author*	*Price (£)*
Adventures in Morocco	J. Rider	1.65
The Jackals of London	Paula Prentice	2.35
The President's Story	J. Arthur Goldman	3.30
Crimson the Blood	C. Storritzer	1.25
The History of Irish Politics	S. O'Leary	4.50
Soldiers Royal	Col P. Oppenheimer	4.75
Ships of the Armada	B. Holt	5.45
The Truth about Holmes	F. Abbott	1.50
The October Revolution	J. Schultz	2.45
Coventry Cathedral	Rev. Arthur Mallett	1.75
Morals and Christianity	James Munn	2.35
Churches in Wales	Alwyn Jones	3.45
The English Cathedrals	Sandra Smith	5.65
The English Martyrs	P. O'Connell	1.55
The Story of Battleships	Admiral George Covey	5.50

The Fleet Air Arm	Admiral George Covey	4.50
The U Boats in World War II	Admiral George Covey	4.25
Buchenwald from the Inside	Hans Gruber	1.60
The Nazi Saga	Karl Auer	2.50
Concentration Camps	L. Brooker	1.85

Invoices

Langham Bookshops, Dover
Bought from
Enterprise Publishers Ltd

Title	*Quantity*	*Price*	*Total*
Ships of the Armada	3		
The English Cathedrals	2		
The Story of Battleships	3		
The History of Irish Politics	1		
Churches in Wales	2		———
less 30% trade discount			———
			═══

Lancashire Books Ltd, Blackburn
Bought from
Enterprise Publishers Ltd

Title	*Quantity*	*Price*	*Total*
The Fleet Air Arm	4		
The Truth about Holmes	1		
Churches in Wales	4		
Crimson the Blood	5		
The Nazi Saga	2		———
less 30% trade discount			———
			═══

A–Z Booksellers Ltd, Leicester
Bought from
Enterprise Publishers Ltd

Title	*Quantity*	*Price*	*Total*
The English Martyrs	2		
The October Revolution	3		
Churches in Wales	5		
Soldiers Royal	1		
Coventry Cathedral	3		
Adventures in Morocco	5		——
less 30% trade discount			
			——
			═══

Gordon & Green, Sunderland
Bought from
Enterprise Publishers Ltd

Title	*Quantity*	*Price*	*Total*
The Jackals of London	11		
The President's Story	2		
Morals and Christianity	5		——
less 30% trade discount			
			——
			═══

A. P. Mitchell (Books) Ltd, Exeter
Bought from
Enterprise Publishers Ltd

Title	*Quantity*	*Price*	*Total*
U Boats in World War II	3		
Buchenwald from the Inside	2		
Concentration Camps	3		——
less 30% trade discount			
			——
			═══

Your task

You are asked to complete the invoices in the same way as Julian would have done. What is the total of the trade discount allowed on these invoices? If you have a pocket calculator, use it to check the calculations.

Questions for discussion by the group

1 Do you think it would be better if the books were numbered in the catalogue? What would the advantages be? And the disadvantages? Can you suggest an improved system of cataloguing?

2 Where does the money go when someone buys a book at a shop? Trace the money as far as you can – identifying as many people as possible who are involved in the production and sale of a book.

6 V. G. ANTIQUES

Victoria Gerrard was once a well-known actress on the West End stage but she found it increasingly difficult to find parts, so she bought herself a business in Charing Cross. She had always been interested in antiques and that is what she decided to deal in. She did very well in her first two years of trading and decided she had earned herself a holiday. But although she had two young ladies who worked for her on a part-time basis, she had no one she could leave in charge of the shop. No one, that is, until her niece, Vanessa, broke up from college. Vanessa was on a business-studies course, and although she was rather young to be left in charge, she was keen and capable. So Victoria spent a couple of weeks with her niece explaining the intricacies of antiques, and then went off for a ten-day holiday in the Canaries.

Before she left Victoria explained the system of pricing she used for the goods in her shop. Attached to each item was a small tag with certain letters on it. These letters represent a code:

V.	G.	A	N	T	I	Q	U	E	S
1	2	3	4	5	6	7	8	9	0

When a customer came into the shop they would have to ask the price of any items they were interested in. Vanessa would then have to look at the price tag and read out the price. If the tag showed NS/TS the price would be £40.50, while a tag with VS/SS on it would indicate a price of £10.00.

During the time she was in charge of the shop Vanessa sold twelve items. She kept the price tags and these are listed below:

China umbrella stand	AT/TS
Minton dinner service	UG/GT
Copper dinner gong	VT/SS
Silver cake dish	AI/TS
Leather-padded footstool	GG/GT
Cut-glass candlesticks	NQ/GS
Spinning-stool	TI/QT
Copper-warming pan	AG/TS
Porcelain figures	VE/AT
Framed oil painting by Valente	GES/SS
Child's Windsor chair	GN/QT
Chinese vase	VE/TS

Her aunt had told her she could reduce the price by 10% if she felt that this would clinch a sale, but Vanessa had only done this in the case of the oil painting and the silver cake dish.

Just before her aunt came back Vanessa paid into the bank the cash and cheques she had received. All the purchasers had paid by cheque except the lady who purchased the dinner gong. Below is the counterfoil for the paying-in slip:

Midchester Bank Ltd
to the credit of Miss V. Gerrard

	(£)
Notes	14.00
Silver	0.90
Copper	0.10
	15.00
Cheques	24.75
	19.35
	32.50

35.50
22.25
261.00
32.65
56.75
82.25
19.15
47.20

£648.35

According to the price tags she should have been able to pay in £648.90. Can you see where the mistakes were made?

Questions for group discussion

1. What is the danger of accepting cheques in payment for goods such as these? How do you think the shopkeepers might protect themselves?
2. Suppose a customer came into the shop and was very interested in a particular item, say an antique ivory chess-set, but the price tag was missing. If this occurred in the middle of Victoria's holiday, how do you think Vanessa should have dealt with the problem?
3. Do you think people prefer to buy goods which have fixed prices, or do they like to bargain?

7 VIVIAN'S VAN HIRE

Vivian Smith took up long-distance lorry-driving when he left the Royal Marines in 1976, but he wanted to set up his own business, and this he did a few weeks ago. He went into partnership with his son, Michael. They bought two small vans, borrowing the money from the bank against the security of Vivian's house. They then put an advertisement in the local press which reads:

Hire-a-Van from Vivian Smith & Son

Day and night service	Have vans – will travel
Reasonable tariffs	Telephone Princewell 762
	(evenings after 6 p.m.)

The Smiths operate a very simple tariff. The charges are based on the (one-way) distance travelled, so that if they are asked to carry a cargo from A to B, a distance of 15 miles, they will charge the customer 55p per kilometre – £8.25 – in accordance with the schedule set out below:

Freight schedule

Short-range trips – up to 15 kilometres – 75p per kilometre
Medium-range trips – 15 to 50 kilometres – 55p per kilometre
Long-range trips – over 50 kilometres – 45p per kilometre

Michael's wife, Paula, deals with telephone calls when she comes home from work in the evenings. She has kept a log of the trips Vivian and Michael have made in the week of operations.

Vivian's log

Monday a.m. Princewell to Bilchester 17km
p.m. nil
Tuesday a.m. Princewell to Pennistone 25km
p.m. Blue Haven to Conniston 57km
Wednesday a.m. Pennistone to Alandale 7km
p.m. nil
Thursday a.m. nil
p.m. Princewell to Charminster 11km
Friday a.m. Blue Haven to Bute Waters 85km
p.m. nil

Michael's log

Monday a.m. Princewell to Gannymede 68km
p.m. Princewell to Lumbwell 96km
Tuesday a.m. Gannymede to Lumbwell 28km
p.m. Princewell to Breconridge 28km
Wednesday a.m. Gannymede to Lumbwell 28km
p.m. nil
Thursday a.m. Princewell to Charminster 11km
p.m. Princewell to Loggerhead 189km
Friday a.m. nil
p.m. Gannymede to Lumbwell 28km

Your first task

Paula's (part-time) job is also to make out invoices to the various customers. How much would she have charged for each of the above trips? What were the total receipts of the business for that first week? If 2/7ths of the receipts were spent on petrol, how much would be left to share between the partners?

Questions for discussion by the group

1 Which is the most popular trip according to the logs kept during the first week? Do you see any problems if this trip continues to be popular? (Study the distances mentioned and the way the charges are compiled).
2 Can you think of any way in which the *freight schedule* could be improved?
3 How do you think the profits should be shared fairly between the partners? (One suggestion is that the profits should be shared in the ratio of 3:2 between Vivian and Michael respectively.)
4 How do you think Paula should be rewarded for the part she plays in the proceedings?

8 CONTESSA GLASSWARE

The Imperial Glass Manufacturing Co. Ltd make a particularly beautiful range of glassware known as 'Contessa'. The Contessa section of Imperial's catalogue reads as follows:

The Contessa range for the connoisseur

	per item	per six
Cut-glass decanter ½-litre size	£37.50	–
full-litre size	48.75	–
,, Sherry glasses	1.35	7.20
,, Wine glasses	1.45	7.75
,, Champagne glasses	1.55	8.25
,, Whisky tumblers	1.25	7.00
,, Brandy glasses	1.65	8.95
,, goblets	9.25	–

Cut-glass fruit dishes	26.75	–
,, paperweights	3.85	22.50
,, ashtrays	7.75	44.65

Note: No special terms are quoted per half dozen when the items are individually packaged and presented.

When Tony Brown joined Imperial Glass his first job was to write up certain invoices which were being sent out to stores which had ordered items from the Contessa range. Some of those invoices are shown below and you are asked to complete them as Tony would have done.

Where the order is for more than 6 items, the first 6 are at the cheap rate and the extra have to be at the rate for single items. So, if the order is for 8 sherry glasses, it is calculated thus:

£7.20 + (2 x £1.35) = £9.90

Imperial Glass Manufacturing Co. Ltd
to Boon's Stores, Grand Parade, Bath

	(£)
3 cut-glass decanters (full-litre size)	
24 sherry glasses	
24 champagne glasses	
3 cut-glass ashtrays	______
add V.A.T. at 8%	
	______
	======

Imperial Glass Manufacturing Co. Ltd
to J. H. Melhuish & Sons, Chelmsford

	(£)
4 cut-glass paperweights	
18 wine glasses	
2 whisky tumblers	
6 cut-glass ½-litre decanters	
3 brandy glasses	______
add V.A.T. at 8%	
	______
	======

Imperial Glass Manufacturing Co. Ltd
to Messrs Barker and Trupp, Wigan

	(£)
2 cut-glass decanters (½-litre size)	
7 cut glass goblets	
12 wine glasses	
12 sherry glasses	
add V.A.T. at 8%	

Imperial Glass Manufacturing Co. Ltd
to Lorrimer's Stores, Bedford

	(£)
4 cut-glass fruit dishes	
12 brandy glasses	
15 wine glasses	
6 cut-glass paperweights	
add V.A.T. at 8%	

Imperial Glass Manufacturing Co. Ltd
to Freeman's Store, High Wycombe

	(£)
18 whisky tumblers	
18 wine glasses	
3 cut-glass decanters (full-litre size)	
8 brandy glasses	
12 cut-glass paperweights	
add V.A.T. at 8%	

When you have completed the invoices check the figures with your pocket calculators. If these are not available, check each other's workings:

(a) What is the total amount of V.A.T. on these invoices?
(b) What are the total receipts from the sale of paperweights on these invoices (inclusive of V.A.T.)?

Questions for the group

1 Why do you think some of the prices in the Contessa range are made more attractive if you buy 6 items at a time? What are the advantages likely to be from the manufacturer's point of view?
2 Do you think the people who buy expensive glassware like this prefer to see their purchases attractively packaged? Or would they sooner have a basic package – and a slight reduction in price?

9 FOOTWEAR FASHIONS

Below are the heights and shoe sizes of a sample of 15 young ladies attending a college of further education in the Midlands:

Name	*Height (in cm)*	*Shoe size*
Annette	163	4½
Belinda	172	6
Caroline	188	7½
Diane	159	5
Erica	178	7
Fiona	167	6
Gina	163	5
Heather	168	5½
Ilsa	173	6
Jane	175	6½
Katie	156	4½
Lorraine	172	6½
Mandy	185	7
Nadia	180	6½
Olga	164	5½

The heights and shoe sizes of the first three girls have been plotted on the special sort of graph shown in Figure 2.1 called a *scatter diagram.* Draw your own graph and complete the remaining plots. Do not join up the plots you mark in.

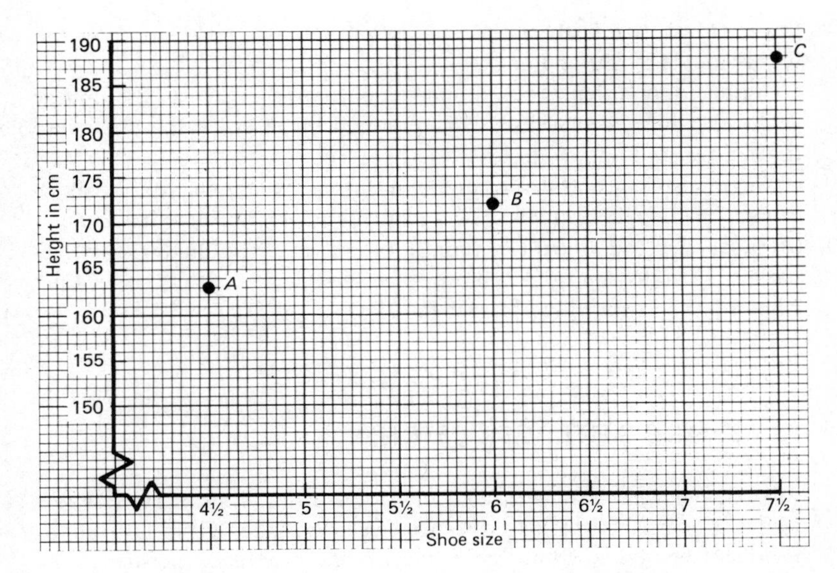

FIGURE 2.1 *Scatter diagram showing relationship between height and shoe sizes*

Your first task

1. Find the average height of the girls in this group (to the nearest cm).
2. Rewrite the list, putting the taller girls first and the shorter girls last.
3. Determine the median height of the girls.
4. What conclusions do you draw from the evidence here?

Your second task (to be considered by the group)

Consider two problems which young Susan Saunders had to face. Susan was the Senior Sales Assistant in a shoe shop on the outskirts of Wolverhampton. Her Manageress had gone on holiday for a fortnight, thus leaving Susan in charge.

Before she had left the Manageress had ordered from Head Office 120 pairs of a new Italian fashion sandal. Unfortunately she had omitted to indicate the different sizes she required. Head Office telephoned

Susan to ask her instructions and she promised to let them know her requirements by the end of the day.

Basing your calculations on the sample of the girls at the college dealt with here, decide how Susan should break down the order into the various sizes and half sizes.

Susan also faced a second problem during the absence of her Manageress. A lady who claimed to be a regular customer brought back a pair of shoes she had bought a month previously. The ankle strap had broken. How do you think Susan should have dealt with the complaint? What are the financial implications?

10 SHANE'S REPRODUCTIONS

Colin Shane was born with a silver spoon in his mouth. He was not particularly bright but his father was wealthy. When Colin left school he tried a few jobs without great success and eventually persuaded his father to give him some capital so that he could go into his own business. Colin was particularly interested in furniture so he bought the lease of a shop on the outskirts of his native Manchester and began to buy reproduction furniture from local furniture-makers. For the uninitiated reproduction furniture is made in the style of a period, but is not antique.

One of the first problems faced by Colin was how to price the furniture he had bought. His father, who owned other businesses, came to his aid.

'Mark it up by a third,' he suggested.

'What does that mean?' asked Colin.

'If it cost you £300,' explained his father, 'one-third of £300 is £100. You add £100 to £300 and sell it for £400.'

Colin thought about this suggestion, but he wanted to concentrate on the more expensive lines, so he devised his own plan, and here it is:

Shane's mark-up for reproduction furniture

Goods costing up to £100 – mark-up by 1/3rd
" " between £100 and £199.99 – mark-up by 3/8ths
" " between £200 and £299.99 – mark-up by 2/5ths
" " above £300 – mark-up by 5/12ths

In the list below you will see the prices paid for his first consignment.

	(£)
Georgian-style cocktail cabinet (yew)	239.00
Writing bureau (mahogany)	189.25
Bookcase (mahogany)	260.00
Georgian-style pedestal desk	179.50
Solid mahogany Pembroke table	549.00
Hand-finished chest of drawers	140.00
Queen Anne style Nest of Tables	52.25
Break-front bookcase (walnut)	550.00
3 hi-fi record cabinets	43.50 each
Davenport desk (Georgian-style)	173.25
Bow-fronted Corner Cabinet (walnut)	98.95
Queen Anne style china cabinet (yew)	263.75
2 mini sofa tables	68.25 each
Solid mahogany serving table	103.00
Georgian-style kneehole desk	205.00

Your instructions come in three parts:

1. Make out a bill as received from his suppliers.

2. Prepare a price list, applying mark-up at the rates quoted.

Colin rounded all selling prices to the nearest £ (if it came to 50p exactly, he took it to the £ above).

3. He had sold all these items within the first month of trading with the exception of the corner cabinet and one of the record cabinets. He decided to reduce the prices of these remaining items by a fifth, and once he had done this they were sold immediately. How much profit had he made at the end of all these transactions?

Questions for the group

1 Colin would like to build up his business on the more expensive items. Do you think his mark-up schedule will help him to do this?

2 If a customer came back to Colin complaining about faulty hinges on the writing bureau, how do you think he should deal with the complaint?

11 THE GUYS AND DOLLS DISCO

Jan Ryder and his sister Sue live on the outskirts of Coventry. For two whole years they fretted that there was very little entertainment for young people in their particular part of town. Then one day they put their heads together and decided to do something about it. They started off by hiring the parish hall. There were some sympathetic councillors who appreciated the problems of young people and they were able to hire the hall for £5 each Saturday evening – except on the rare occasions when it was required for political meetings.

Jan and Sue then made some enquiries and found they could hire disc jockeys who would bring their own equipment and records or tapes along for a fee. Some bookings were made – well in advance – and then the brother and sister began to organise the publicity. Sue was convinced there would be many more boys than girls wanting to come, so they decided on a novel arrangement. There would be blue tickets for the boys at 65p each, and pink tickets for the girls at 45p each. Jan felt that, in view of the coloured tickets, 'the Guys and Dolls Disco' would be an apt name for the venture.

The attendances of the first six discotheques are shown below:

Tickets sold	*Guys*	*Dolls*
Saturday, 1 February	94	35
8	83	34
22	62	32
8 March	71	36
22	85	42
29	69	38

At the end of the month Jan decided to check up to see how they were doing financially. Sue provided him with the bills from the disc jockeys. They still had these to pay:

1 February	Alberto John – £18.50
8	Peter and Paul – £15.00
22	Miss Scotland – £17.75
8 March	Charlie Ross – £22.00
22	Zebidee McCaul £25.00
29	Marty Mild – £14.50

Your first task

1 Calculate which of the disc jockeys produced the biggest profit for the Guys and Dolls Disco.
2 What was the average attendance of (a) guys, and (b) dolls at these first six discos?

Your second task

Using the information given so far you are asked to complete the statement below for Jan and Sue.

Guys and Dolls Disco for February and March

		(£)
Receipts from sale of tickets	Guys	
	Dolls	______
less cost of hiring hall		______
less cost of disc jockeys		______
less cost of tickets and posters		3.76
	Net receipts	======

Questions for the group to discuss

1 Jan feels there are still too few girls coming to the disco. What could be done to change the situation?
2 Sue would like to book the famous disc jockey Brook Paterson, but he is asking a fee of £50. She still thinks it would be a good idea because she reckons the number of girls attending would be doubled. How would this affect the receipts and profit?
3 Some of the previously sympathetic councillors have been concerned at damage done to the hall at a recent disco, and in future the fee for hiring the hall is going to be increased to £15. How do you think Sue and Jan might react? Would this make the disco run at a loss?

12 BUYRITE SUPERMARKETS

It was Friday night and the supermarket was full. Michael Stiles, the young Assistant Manager, was settling down to his new job very nicely. It was only his first week at the Wolverhampton branch but already he was feeling that he 'belonged'. He looked at the clock. One hour to closing time. Little did he realise the variety of problems which were going to confront him during that time.

First, there was the incident with the little old lady. Michael spotted her near the toiletries shelves. He was going over to see if he could help her. She seemed in some sort of difficulty. But as he approached he saw she was slipping sachets of hair shampoo into an inside pocket of her overcoat. He signalled to the Manager and before he arrived the dear little old lady was helping herself to tubes of cream cheese. From then on the Manager took over the problem, ushering the culprit into his office.

Shortly after, a policewoman appeared and was also shown into the office. The Manager put his head round the door.

'Michael,' he called, 'spare me a minute will you.' He introduced Michael to the policewoman, to whom all this was obviously routine. 'Just make a list of all the items we found in this lady's pockets,' he said.

Michael was surprised at the size of the pile. By the time he had finished the list looked like this:

		(£)
4 tins of anchovies at 79p each	=	
5 tubes of cream cheese at 53p each	=	
3 jars of honey at 68p each	=	
12 sachets of hair shampoo at 24p each	=	
7 tins of saccharine at 48p each	=	
9 tubes of toothpaste at 39p each	=	
3 packets of jelly at 19p each	=	
17 bath cubes at 11p each	=	______
		======

'How much does it come to?' asked the Manager.

Michael was on the point of taking the list to one of the cashiers but that was not possible. All the lanes had queues of people waiting to be dealt with and – putting even more pressure on him – the attractive young policewoman was smiling in a way that suggested she thought the task of performing the calculations might be beyond him.

He worked out the total and then turned to the policewoman.

'Would you like to check it for me?' he asked.

It was her turn to look uncomfortable.

But Michael's day was by no means over.

'Oh! Michael,' said the Manager, 'while I am tied up here will you go out and reduce all the perishables – by 15%.'

Michael resolved to bring his pocket calculator with him in future, but for the moment he had to work out the new prices unaided – stating the price both per kilo and per lb where appropriate.

	Original price	*New price*
Bananas (per lb)	30p	
(per kilo)	66p	
Rainbow trout (per lb)	115p	
(per kilo)	253p	
Grapes (per lb)	70p	
(per kilo)		
Minced beef (per lb)	85p	
(per kilo)		
Cartons of cream (300g)	57p	

You will see that someone had rubbed out the prices per kilo of the grapes and the minced beef, but Michael has all the information he needs for his task.

When he had completed this task the Manager appeared again. Michael was just going to ask him how the shoplifting incident had ended, when a young housewife cut in front of him and confronted the Manager. She held up two packets of Topaz washing powder.

'Which is the best buy?' she asked, 'I can't work it out,'

In the one hand she held a packet which offered 870g (30.7oz) for 58p. In the other hand she held a packet offering 810g (28.5oz) for 48p.

The Manager did not hesitate.

'The larger packet is the better value,' he said.

Was he right?

Your first task

Working in groups of twos or threes, perform the calculations which Michael would have been required to make.

Questions for discussion by the group

1. What do you think Michael should have done if he thought the Manager had misinformed the customer?
2. How do you think stores should deal with the problem of pilfering? Who bears the cost of pilfering?

13 THE STRATFORD BEACON

Jill Anderson works for the local newspaper, the *Stratford Beacon*, and her job is to calculate the costs of the various advertisements which appear in the weekly editions. On page 3 advertisers are allowed to choose any size of block, and the costing schedules are shown below:

Block advertisements

Industrial and commercial firms	65p per sq.cm
Educational bodies and charities	52p per sq cm
All others	60p per sq.cm.

In Figure 2.2 a selection of advertisements for the next edition are displayed. An example of the calculation that Jill needs to make is given here.

Using the scale shown, the block for the Grasshopper Disco measures 5 cm x 2 cm. That gives an area of 10 sq. cm:

10 x 65p = £6.50

The costs calculated by Jill then have to be written on to the *cost schedule* below. You are asked to calculate the costs and complete the schedule – bearing in mind that where there is a repeat advertisement (i.e. one which goes into more than one edition), there is a 20% reduction in the charge.

Cost schedule

	Area (sq. cm)	Rate (p)	Cost (£)
The Grasshopper Disco	10	65	6.50
Club Chandelles		65	
Seafood Restaurant (repeat)		65	

Oxfam	52	
Stratford Technical College	52	
The Trivoli Ballroom (repeat)	65	
Stratford Athletic Club	60	
Pandella Off-Licence		
White Hart Inn (repeat)	65	
Tim Cheng's Take-Away	60	
Stratford Ratepayers' Association	60	
Bloomfield's Electronics	65	
The Pavlova Ballet School (repeat)	65	______
		======

Jill must check the list to see whether there are any omissions or mistakes.

Questions for the group

1 Why do you think the *Stratford Beacon* charges different rates to business advertisers? Who do you think should be treated preferentially? Be specific and give reasons.

2 Do you think a newspaper is simply another profit-making organisation – or are there social responsibilities to be brought into account?

A task for the group

Each student should select three widely differing newspapers and analyse and compare the contents. What percentage of the area of each newspaper is devoted to each of the following subject areas?

	%age
Photographs (excluding those in advertisements)	
Advertisements	
International news items	
Sports	
Financial news	
Fashion	
Remainder	
	100%

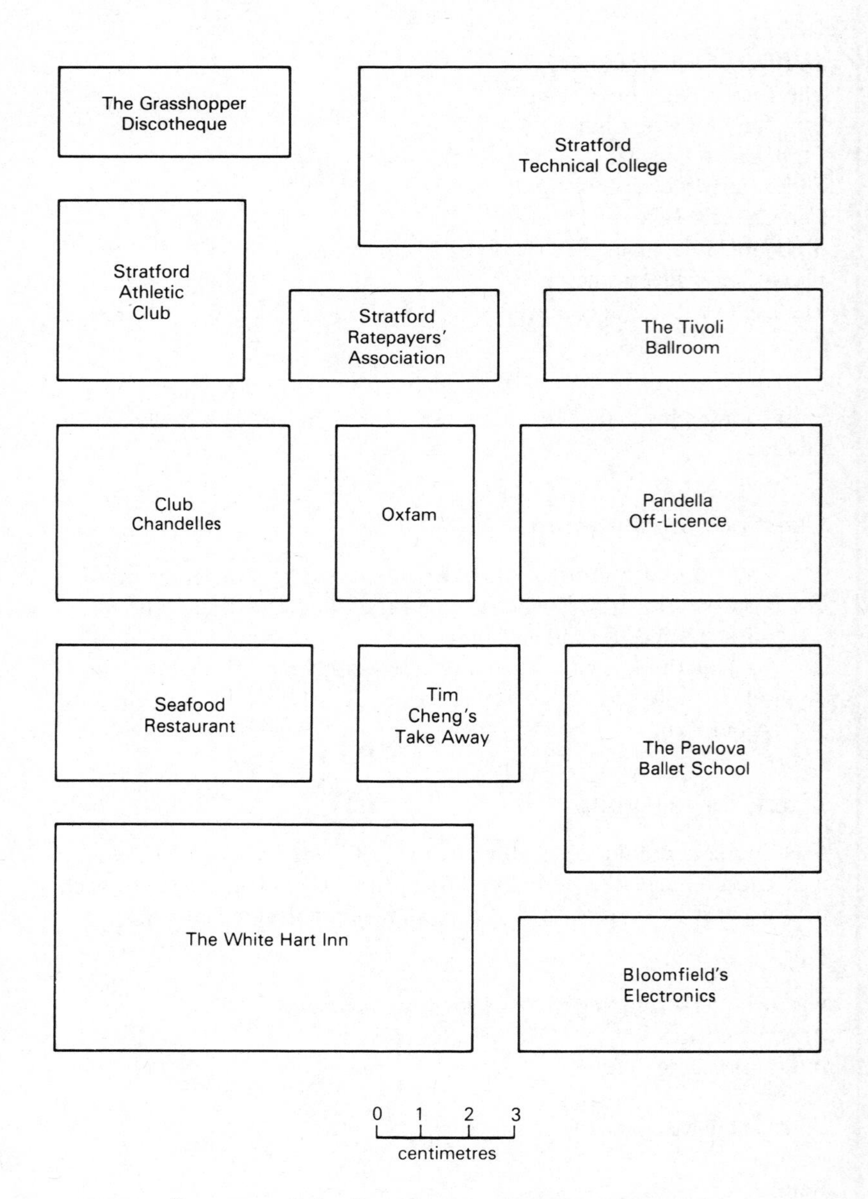

FIGURE 2.2 *Page 3 of the 'Stratford Beacon'*

When each student has completed his/her individual research, come together and compare notes. What conclusions have you reached?

14 SLATTERY MIRRORS

Dan and Chris Slattery have inherited their father's business. The firm sells mirrors. The mirrors are sold to retailers. They are unframed and are of three qualities. They are priced according to their area:

Super Quality sells at £21.50 per sq. metre
Extra Quality ,, ,, £13.60 per sq. metre
Standard Quality ,, ,, £11.20 per sq. metre

Occasionally they sell to members of the public but when this happens the customer is not given the 25% trade discount.

Here is a selection of invoices and you are asked to complete the details.

Invoice
(to Howard's Hardware)

		(£)
Standard Quality	2m × 1m	
	1.5m × 2m	
Extra Quality	1.4m × 0.4m	
Super Quality	2.2m × 0.5m	______
	less 25% trade discount	
		______
	add 8% V.A.T.	
		______
		======

Invoice
(to Gant Hill Stores)

		(£)
Super Quality	0.7m × 0.5m	
Standard Quality	2m × 1.6m	
	1.2m × 2.1m	
	0.9m × 0.9m	
Extra Quality	0.5m × 0.8m	______
	less 25% trade discount	
		______
	add 8% V.A.T.	
		______
		======

Invoice
(to Mr P. Prendergast)

		(£)
Extra Quality	1.55m x 0.3m	
	2.5m x 0.35m	
	add 8% V.A.T.	

Invoice
(to James Spragg Ltd)

		(£)
Standard Quality	1.1m x 1.1m	
	0.6m x 4.25m	
	0.9m x 0.9m	
	2.35m x 1.5m	
Extra Quality	2.4m x 1.9m	
Super Quality	0.2m x 0.3m	
	less 25% trade discount	
	add 8% V.A.T.	

If you have a pocket calculator available, you can use it to check your workings.

The brothers trade in the form of a partnership and have wisely drawn up a *partnership deed* which lays down that Dan is to take 9 parts of the profit while Chris takes 5 parts. In other words, 9/14ths of the profit goes to Dan and 5/14ths to Chris. If last year the profits amounted to £2934.86 and this year they rose to £4765.98, how much would the brothers have received as their share of the profit?

For group discussion

1 Why do you think one partner takes so much more of the profits than the other? What explanations might there be?
2 Do you think it fair that the Slatterys give retailers a 25% trade discount which they deny to their other customers?

15 SWISS BREAKFAST FOOD

West Country Foods Ltd introduced a new breakfast food on to the market some six months ago. It is made up of roasted wheatflakes, sultanas, nuts and shredded dried apple, and is marketed under the name of 'Morning Sunshine – Swiss Style Breakfast Food.' West Country Foods are selling the product in five different-sized packets. The price is related directly to the weight of the packets, so that the kilogram packet, for example, is exactly twice as expensive as the 500-gram packet. Bearing this in mind you are asked to complete the table below (the recommended price for sale to the public is 30% higher than the wholesale price which West Country Foods obtain from the retail shops and supermarkets):

	Weight packet	Wholesale price	Retail price
Giant Family Size	1kg	£1.20	£1.56
Family Size	500g		
Economy Size	375g		
Standard Size	275g		
Small Size	175g		

In the next table you will find the value of the sales of the new product during the first six months of its 'life'. Your next task is to complete the plots on Figure 2.3. The first two plots have already been made for you.

Monthly sales of Morning Sunshine

Month	Sales (£000)
March	17.5
April	20.0
May	25.0
June	27.5
July	32.5
August	37.5

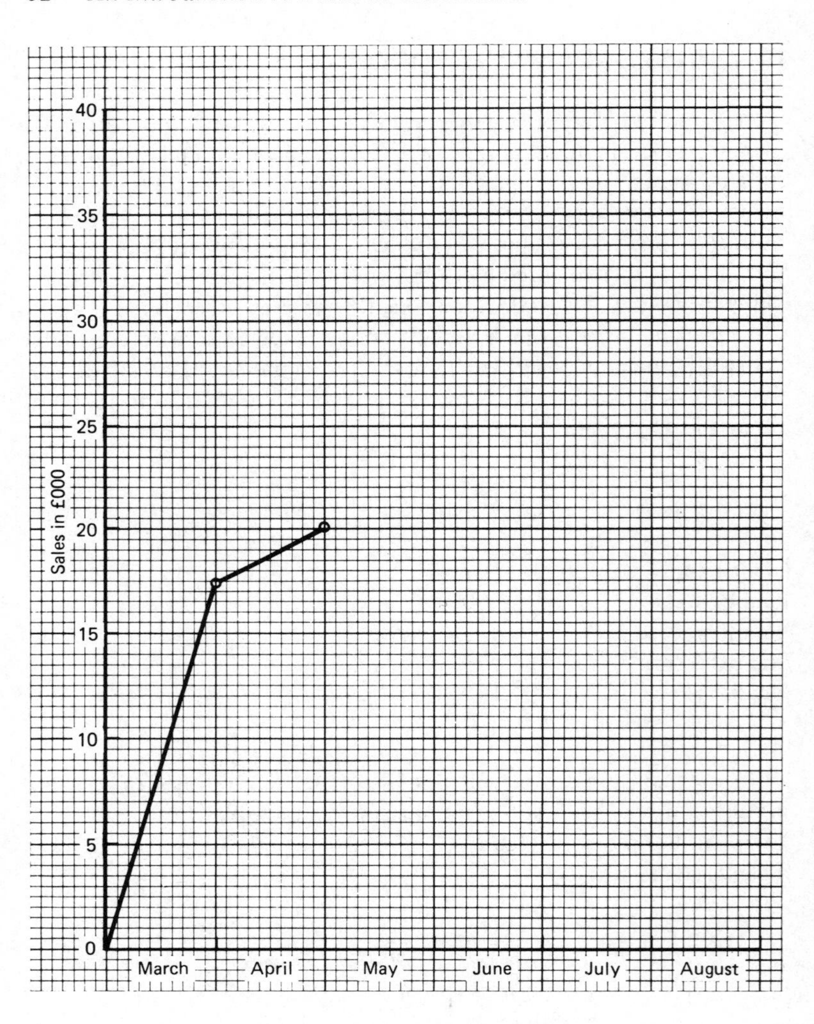

FIGURE 2.3 *Sales of Morning Sunshine*

Now use all the information provided to answer the following questions:

1 What are the average monthly sales to date?
2 What are the average monthly sales over the last three months?
3 On the evidence here, what do you think the sales would be in September?

4 How much larger is the Economy Size than the Small Size?

Questions for group discussion

1 Do you think the purchasers will expect to buy the larger packets more cheaply? Why do you think they would expect this benefit? How much would you expect to reduce the larger packets by? Be as specific as you can.
2 Do you think the public prefer products like this to be attractively packaged – even if it puts the price up? What are the arguments in favour and against?

16 BURTON UNITED

Even since Burton United reached the Third Round of the F.A. Cup last year they have been looking for a ground of their own. Their record in the Fourth Division this year has been impressive (they have scored 16 goals in the first three games of the season) and this has maintained their enthusiasm. Until now they have been leasing a ground from a local brewery, but the lessors want to develop the site for a hotel and office block. Fortunately for the club one of the directors Julian Wormsley, has some parcels of land in the locality which he is prepared to offer the club at favourable prices. The rest of the Board of Directors agree that the choice rests between three options and, since these plots are equally acceptable otherwise, they will choose the cheapest of the alternatives.

Option 1

This is called Broomfield and is on the northern outskirts of the town. The shape of the plot is shown in Figure 2.4.

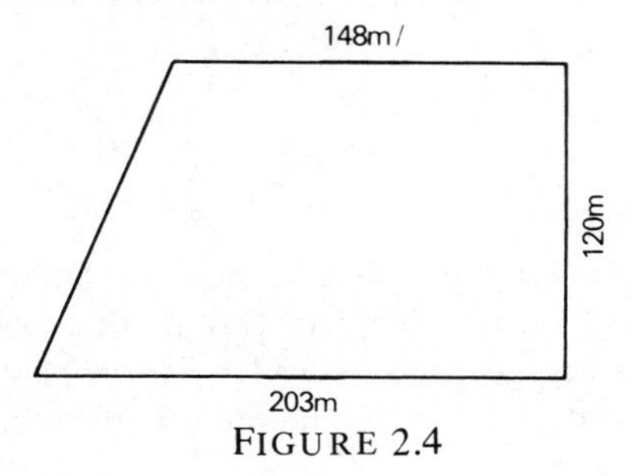

FIGURE 2.4

Wormsley is offering this plot at £2.00 per sq. metre. (Note: in order to find the area of a right-angled triangle you multiply the base length by the height and divide the answer by 2. The formula is $(b \times h)/2$.)

Option 2

This piece of land used to be a smallholding owned by the Fletcher family. The surviving member of the family sold up recently and emigrated to New Zealand. The land has always been known as Fletcher's Hollow. It is rectangular in shape and measures 150 x 120 metres. Wormsley is offering it to Burton United at £1.95 per sq. metre.

Option 3

This land is close to the centre of town and is known as The Open Market. Until recently there used to be stalls on the site selling a wide range of merchandise – from dress materials to assorted cheeses. The land offered is a perfect square measuring 130 metres on each side. Wormsley is offering this site at £2.05 per sq. metre.

Your first task

Decide which plot of land is cheapest.

Questions for the group

Bearing in mind that the directors are planning to contruct a football pitch 120 metres long and 70 metres wide, how would you expect to find the pitch placed on the plot? Where would the stands be built – and why there?

A further task

At the end of the season the club sold their star striker, Ian Morrison, to a famous First Division club. As part of the deal Burton are to receive £175 for every goal scored by Ian for his new club during his first season with them. So far he has netted the following goals:

Against Liverpool 1 goal
,, Norwich 2 goals
,, Manchester City 3 goals
,, Leeds United 2 goals
,, Arsenal 1 goal

How much is due to Burton United from this part of the deal so far? Last year Ian scored 28 goals for Burton United. How much would the club receive if he repeated this performance for his new club?

Further questions for the group

1 How do you think the value of a football star can be calculated?
2 Why do you think football managers get sacked by their clubs when the teams fail to win games?
3 What is the difference between football and any other business?

17 THE SURF-SKATERS

Although Simon Hepplewaite is still in his teens, he is making quite a name for himself as an inventor. His first invention of note was a breathing device which allowed a swimmer to stay underwater while connected to the surface by a simple plastic tube leading to a rubber buoy. It did not sell in England very well but there were substantial sales in the New World. His latest invention looks like being an even bigger money-spinner. He has produced what might be described as a cross between a skateboard and a surfboard for use on land. It consists of a simple reinforced circular disc 2 centimetres thick which has six skate wheels attached to it. The novelty is that the skate wheels are designed to rotate freely in any direction, with the result that the surf-skater is able to gyrate while he is in motion to a much greater extent than with the old-fashioned skateboards.

Simon has found a manufacturer to produce his invention on a large scale. Sales have been so good that, although the first Surf Skates were produced for youngsters, the manufacturer now wants to produce larger ones for the adult market. He is confident that the craze will catch on.

The first Surf Skates – now called 'Junior Skates' – had a 25 cm radius and were sold to retailers at £22.50 each. The manufacturer has decided to produce two new sizes which he describes as:

Senior Skates – with a radius of 35cm
Giant Skates – with a radius of 50cm

He is going to charge the retailers the same price per sq. cm for the new versions – so that if the Senior Skates have twice the surface area of the Junior Skates, then they will cost twice the price to the retailer.

Your first task

Working in groups of twos or threes, calculate the price the manufacturer will sell the Senior Skates and the Giant Skates to the retailers. A little careful thought can save you a lot of work here.
(*Note*: the formula for finding the area of a circle is
πr^2, where $\pi = 3^1/_7$ or 3.1416.)

Your second task

Assume that we have now moved six months on. The sales are represented in the following table, which shows the numbers sold:

	Junior	Senior	Giant
September	7132	–	–
October	3186	–	–
November	2734	1523	729
December	2345	2674	483
January	1156	1034	97
February	743	735	19

Still working in small groups, answer the following questions:

1 If Simon collects commission of 2½% on all sales, how much has he earned from the sale of Surf Skates for the six months in question?
2 Which month was the best month for sales – in value, and *not* numbers?

Questions for discussion by the full group

1 How do you interpret the sales figures? How could you explain falling sales even though the craze was catching on?
2 How do you think the manufacturer might increase the sales of Surf Skates?

18 THE RAILWAY TIME-TABLE

Gillian Harris lives at Barfield and has a secretarial post at Kingsbury. She had a chance of a job locally but decided to go for a better-paying job 'in town'. Gillian likes clothes and they have to be paid for. You see below the time-table which gives details of the train service which she uses:

Train service from Princeton to Kingsbury

(Weekdays ex. Sat.)

	a.m.	a.m.	a.m.	a.m.	a.m.	a.m.
Princeton	7.32	7.40	7.45	7.52	8.13	8.22
Crannock	7.43	–	7.58	–	–	8.34
Barfield	7.50	–	8.05	–	–	8.42
Durleston	–	–	8.18	8.20	–	8.57
Deer's Leap	8.14	8.18		8.32	–	9.09
Bloxford	8.24	8.27		8.40	9.00	9.20
Kingsbury	8.30	8.33		8.48	9.06	9.26

The questions to answer

1 Which is the latest train that Gillian will be able to catch in order to arrive at her office by 9.00 a.m.?
(Her office is a ten-minute walk away from the station.)
2 What is the average time taken for a journey between Barfield and Kingsbury – according to the trains shown here?
3 Which is the fastest train, and which is the slowest, among those shown?
4 If the 7.40 averages 90 kilometres per hour between Princeton and Deer's Leap, how far is it in kilometres between the two stations?

5 Gillian's boy-friend, David, lives in Princeton. He also works in Kingsbury, but his office is 20 minutes from the station. Does this mean they cannot travel on the same train? (Note that he also has to start work by 9 a.m.)

Gillian has met one of her best friends from school, Joanna Box, and is delighted to hear that she is coming to work in the same office next week. Joanna lives at Deer's Leap and is concerned to know how much the fare is going to be.

'I pay £10.75 for a weekly season ticket,' says Gillian, 'but I don't know how much it would be from Deer's Leap.'

'I'd just like a rough idea,' says Joanna thoughtfully, 'you don't know how far it is, do you?'

'I'm afraid not.'

Joanna brightened: 'I think I know how to get an idea,' she said, 'we've got the time-table, haven't we.'

Do you see what Joanna was getting at? If so, you should be able to work out the sort of price she would have to pay for a weekly season ticket.

Two more questions

1 One of the research assistants in the Traffic Manager's Department has estimated that the average number of passengers travelling on the 8.22 last week was 137. How many passengers in all travelled on the 8.22 last week?
2 If Gillian's take-home pay is £43.00 a week, what proportion of her take-home pay is spent on the weekly season ticket?

Questions for group discussion

1 If it is expensive to travel, why do so many people live away from their jobs? What are the financial advantages and disadvantages?
2 What advantages and disadvantages do railways have compared with other forms of transport?

19 STOCK CONTROL

The first day at a new firm is always an anxious one and when Pauline Pritchard joined the Head Office of Stachwell's Office Supplies Ltd as a stock clerk she wondered what the day would bring. In fact she was allocated to the Stock Control Department in the warehouse. The function of the department was to ensure that adequate stocks were available to meet their customers' requirements. Pauline's Manager was a rather pleasant young man in his early thirties, James Burdett. Having shown her around the warehouse and introduced her to the other members of staff, he took her to the desk which had been allocated to her.

'Have a look at these stock-control cards,' he said, 'and, if you can follow how they work, bring them up to date.'

He explained that she would have to transfer the entries on the Control Sheet for the previous day to the various stock cards in front of her.

'It shouldn't be too difficult,' he said, 'there were only a dozen or so entries on Friday. Write them up and I'll check them when I get back.'

Pauline was very concerned to show that she was an intelligent young lady and scrutinised the Control Sheet and the four Stock Cards her new boss had laid out for her:

Control Sheet – Friday, 30 April

1 Ordered 50 Photocopiers from Quintex
2 Sent 36 Swivel Chairs (F3652) to York branch
3 Sent 180 Quintex Staplers to Grimsby
4 Received 500 Filing Cases (B6642) from Verdex
5 Sent 16 Quintex Photocopiers (E5766) to Reading
6 Sent 50 Quintex Staplers to Salisbury
7 Sent 3 Swivel Chairs to Salisbury
8 Received 60 Quintex Photocopiers from manufacturers
9 Sent 12 Swivel Chairs (F3652) to Weston-Super-Mare
10 Sent 100 Quintex Staplers to Wolverhampton
11 Sent 60 Filing Cases (B6642) to Wolverhampton
12 Sent 6 Quintex Photocopiers to Poole
13 3 Swivel Chairs (F3652) returned from Bristol (unsold and undamaged)
14 Sent 120 Quintex Staplers (E3873) to Bristol
15 Sent 6 Quintex Photocopiers (E5766) to Swindon
16 Sent 50 Quintex Staplers to Newcastle
17 Sent 1 Swivel Chair to Newcastle

Commodity: Bell Swivel Chairs						
Re-order level 72			Catalogue no. F3652			
Date in or out	In from or out to	Stock in	Stock out	Balance	Re-order date	Re-order amount
17/4	b/f			115		
22/4	Bath		23	92		
28/4	Reading		13	79		

Commodity: Quintex Staplers						
Re-order level 360			Catalogue no. E3873			
Date in or out	In from or out to	Stock in	Stock out	Balance	Re-order date	Re-order amount
2/4	b/f			360		
19/4	Grimsby		60	300	22/4	600
22/4	Bath		120	180		
28/4	Quintex	600		780		

Commodity: Filing Cases						
Re-order level 200			Catalogue no. B6642			
Date in or out	In from or out to	Stock in	Stock out	Balance	Re-order date	Re-order amount
17/4	b/f			280		
19/4	Grimsby		60	220		
22/4	Lincoln		60	160	22/4	500
28/4	Luton		36	124		

Commodity: Quintex Photocopiers						
Re-order level 36			Catalogue no. E5766			
Date in or out	In from or out to	Stock in	Stock out	Balance	Re-order date	Re-order amount
10/4	b/f			28		
18/4	Quintex	60		88		
22/4	Bath		18	70		
24/4	Brighton		40	30	24/4	60

Your task

First write-up the stock-control cards for Pauline. As you are doing this you should study the cards critically. Are all the sections necessary? Are any more sections called for? For example, should there be a space for 'Maximum stocks to be held'?
Next, work out the total value of the stock in hand for the four items covered by these stock cards. You are informed by James Burdett that the items are to be valued as follows:

Photocopiers	£60.50 each
Staplers	£2.50 each
Swivel Chairs	£82.25 each
Filing Cases	£3.65 each

Questions for group discussion

1 What are the arguments in favour of carrying ample stocks of the various items?
2 What are the arguments against carrying unnecessarily large stocks?
3 How do you think James Burdett will try to keep the right amount of stock?
4 If you had been in Pauline's shoes, what sort of questions would you have asked the Manager on his return?

20 NEVADA NIGHT RIDE

Nevada Night Ride are a country and western group who have recently gained a following with their distinctive style of entertainment, which is a combination of visual humour and musical talent. They have made three records to date, and although their records have not made the charts they have come close enough to maintain the interest of the recording company, Denton Discs.

Denton Discs have sent the group's agent, George Graham, a pictorial presentation to let them see how well they have done in the first six months of their contract. You will see on the first bar chart (Figure 2.5) the sales from their first three discs to date, and from the second chart (Figure 2.6) you will see how the sales are divided between the United Kingdom, the United States and the Continent (the E.E.C.).

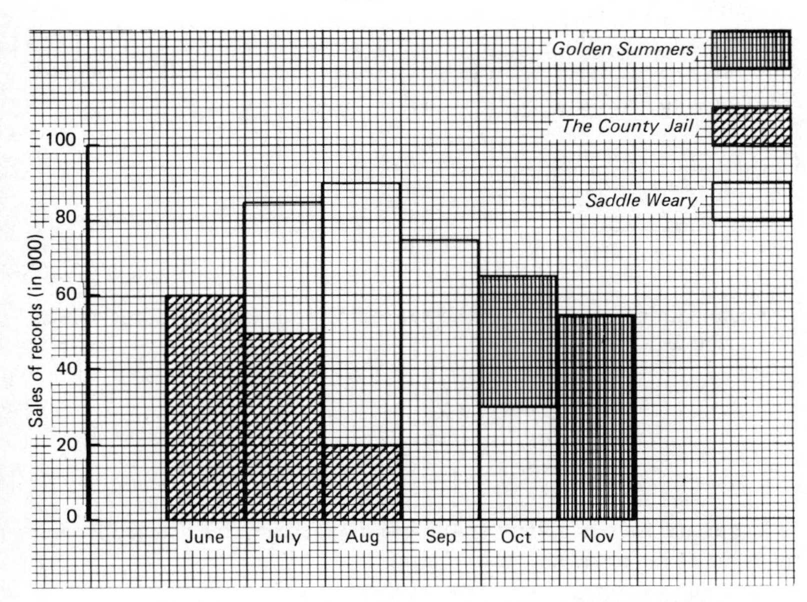

FIGURE 2.5 *Sales of Records by Nevada Night Ride*

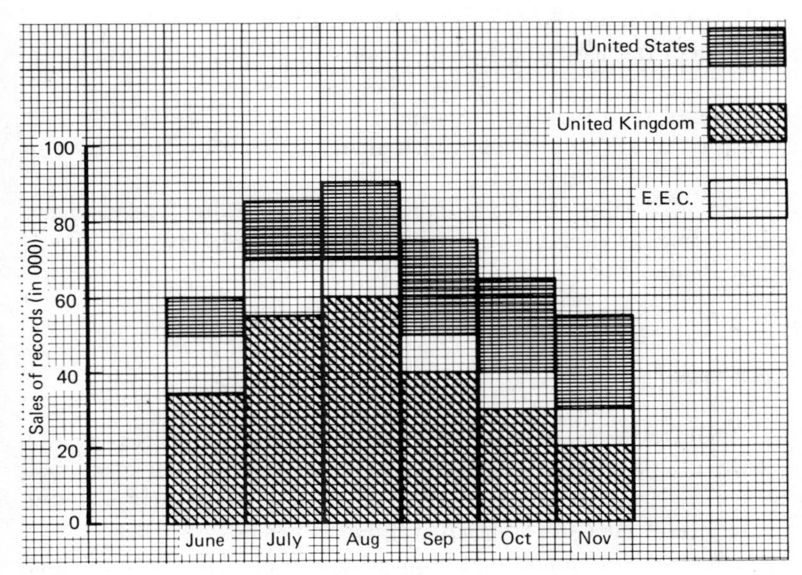

FIGURE 2.6 *Nevada Night Ride: Sales by Area*

A cheque is on the way to the group, but until it arrives they have only these diagrams to indicate how much the cheque will be for. The contract with Denton Discs gives the following royalties.

Calculated on each title taken separately
2½% on first 50,000
3½% on next 50,000
5% on all over 100,000

The calculations are based on the net selling price of the records, which are as follows:

The County Jail	85p
Saddle Weary	87p
Golden Summers	88p

There are four members of the group, and they take the following shares in all the proceeds:

Buddy Holloway (the lead singer) takes 35% of net earnings
Chuck Ryan (the lead guitarist) takes 25% ,, ,, ,,
Anne Stewart (the female singer) takes 20% ,, ,, ,,
Stuart Dalgleish (the drummer) takes 20% ,, ,, ,,

However, before the proceeds are distributed to the group, the agent is entitled to his commission, which amounts to 7½% of the net earnings.

Figure 2.7 (the pie chart) shows the breakdown of sales to the E.E.C. countries (based on the number of records sold in the six-month period in question).

Your tasks

1. Calculate the amount of the cheque which the group can expect from Denton Discs before the agent's commission is deducted.
2. Calculate the amount which each member of the group can expect to receive when the proceeds are apportioned between them.
3. Calculate the proportion of the records sold in the United States over the six-month period.

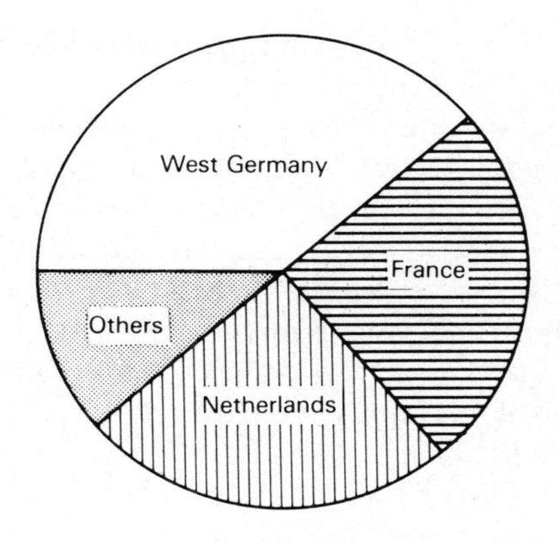

FIGURE 2.7

4 Calculate how many records have been sold in (a) West Germany, and (b) The Netherlands over the six-month period.

(Note: when you see the word 'net' it infers that there are various sums which have been deducted from the figure shown; 'gross' indicates the figure before any deductions are made.)

For group discussion

Denton Discs are trying to persuade the Nevada Night Ride to sign a new contract which will use a different basis for calculating future royalties. Instead of the existing gradated rates, the group would receive 3p for each record sold regardless of price. What advice would you give the group?

21 SPREADEAGLE SPORTS

Charlotte Aldridge thought she was in for trouble when her Manager, Malcolm Stringer, called her into his office. She tried hard to work out what she had done wrong, but she soon realised Malcolm was far from being on the rampage.

'Charlotte,' he said, smiling brightly, 'you got an O-level in Art, if I remember right.'

Charlotte nodded and tried not to look too surprised at the conversation. It turned out that Malcolm had been asked to reproduce some statistics about the firm, Spreadeagle Sports, in a visual form, and he wanted Charlotte's ideas on the subject. Charlotte would have pointed out that her course in Business Calculations at the local technical college was more use on an assignment like this, but thought better of it. She knew her Manager was looking at staff salaries very shortly, and she was hoping for a substantial increase.

Malcolm gave her three sets of figures and asked her to let him have her ideas the following day:

Sales in £m. last year

	Clothing	Equipment
Tennis	1.3	1.9
Football	0.2	2.5
Athletics	0.4	1.7
Hockey	0.5	0.9
Swimming	2.3	0.2

In addition there were sales of 'Miscellaneous Items' not included in the above. 'Miscellaneous Clothing' sales amounted to £347654 and 'Miscellaneous Equipment' sales totalled £461324.

Spreadeagle sell many of their products overseas and Malcolm produces the following breakdown for Charlotte:

Overseas sales for last year (in £000)

South America	223
Scandinavia	154
Rest of Europe	487
United States and Canada	146
Elsewhere	16

As you can see, these figures do not distinguish between Clothing and Equipment.

The final information given is about the work-force and not the products. It shows the composition of the work-force. There is just the one factory – on the outskirts of London.

Composition of work-force by age, sex and department (at 31 Dec last)

		Ages in years			
		less than 27	27 to 36	over 37	Total
Factory	Male	236	217	58	
	Female	312	142	117	
Sales	Male	12	42	17	
	Female	11	7	9	
Personnel	Male	2	6	5	
	Female	7	7	3	
Accounts	Male	5	3	7	
	Female	3	2	0	
Total (of both sexes)					

Your task

Produce the bar charts, pie charts or other diagrams you think Charlotte might have provided for her Manager the next day. When you have completed this task come together and compare your offerings, deciding which visual presentation of the statistics is the most effective. Then work independently again and answer the following questions.

1 What percentage of the work-force is, respectively, male, female, employed in the factory, and under the age of 27?
2 What percentage of total sales was made overseas?
3 What percentage of the sales of *equipment* was related to Football?

Questions for group discussion

1 What are the advantages of selling goods overseas as compared with selling them in the home market, and what are the dangers?
2 Would you prefer to work in a small organisation or a large one, and what are the arguments for and against?

22 HIRE-PURCHASE

It was Susan Coburn's first day at MacDonnell's Department Store and she was put into the Accounts Department. She was guided by Jill

Garner, who was a few years older and had spent six months in the store. One of the jobs they had to do was to work out the payments required under hire-purchase agreements. Customers were able to take delivery of goods they had purchased, after payment of a deposit. They paid for the balance of the purchase price plus interest over a period of 12 months, 18 months or 24 months.

Jill showed Susan the calculations which were required when a hire-purchase account was being dealt with:

Step 1 How much is the cash price? Say, £300. If £30 is paid as a deposit and the rate of interest is 15% per annum, then for a two-year agreement the interest will be equal to £270 x 15/100 x 2 = £81.

Step 2

Cash price + interest	=	£381
less 10% deposit	=	30
Amount outstanding	=	£351

Step 3 Spread over 24 months the hire-purchase instalments would be £351/24 = £14.63 per month.

Step 4 24 payments of £14.63 equals a total of £351.12 (any shortfall or overpayment will be adjusted on the last payment).

After Jill had explained what was required, she let Susan work out a few transactions on her own. You are asked to fill in the missing figures for her.

Transaction 1

A Mr Lattimer has bought a Japanese colour television set on hire-purchase. The cash price was £420 and the payments are to be spread over 18 months:

		(£)
Cash price	=	
less 10% deposit	=	

add interest at 15% = ______

Outstanding amount = ______

This can be paid in 17 instalments of ______
and a final instalment of ______

Transaction 2

Penny Fletcher bought a cassette tape-recorder. The cash price would have been £62, but she decided to buy it on hire-purchase over a term of 12 months:

(£)

Cash price =
less 10% deposit = ______

add interest at 15% = ______

Outstanding amount = ______

This can be paid in 11 instalments of ______
and a final instalment of ______

Transaction 3

Dennis Peebles bought a cine-camera and projector. The cash price was £425, which was much more than he had available in cash, so he bought the equipment on hire-purchase, the payments to be spread over 24 months:

(£)

Cash price =
less 10% deposit = ______

add interest at 15% = ______

Outstanding amount = ______

This can be paid in 23 instalments of ______
and a final instalment of ______

Transaction 4

Mrs A. Polowski purchased a Spreadeagle Tennis Raquet. The cash price would have been £57.75 but Mrs Polowski has asked for a six-month agreement:

		(£)
Cash price	=	
less 10% deposit	=	______
add interest at 15%	=	______
Outstanding amount	=	______
This can be paid in 5 instalments of		______
and a final instalment of		______

Transaction 5

Mr M. Travers bought a dart board which was offered at £18.25 for cash. He asks to pay for it over six months:

		(£)
Cash price	=	
less 10% deposit	=	______
add interest at 15%	=	______
Outstanding amount	=	______
This can be paid in 5 instalments of		______
and a final instalment of		______

Questions for the group to discuss

1 What are the advantages and disadvantages of buying goods on hire purchase (a) from the purchaser's point of view, and (b) from the retailer's point of view?

2 Can you anticipate any special problems for Dennis Peebles with his particular purchases?

3 Do you think the interest charges should be calculated more fairly? (Note that they are based on the total amount borrowed, even though this balance is reduced each month.)

23 HOUSEHOLD EXPENSES

Each property in the country is given a rateable value and it is this figure which is used as a base by the local authority claiming rates from the occupier of the property. How are the rates calculated? If the rateable value is £120 and the rates fixed by the local authority are 50p in the £, the amount to be paid will be:

(50/100)p × £120 = 60 p.a., or £30 per half year

Here are some more rates for you to calculate:

1 Phil Davis has a two-bedroomed bungalow in Gloucester. If the bungalow has a rateable value of £300 and the rates have been fixed by the local authority at 60p in the £, how much will he have to pay for rates every year?
2 Alan Crawford has a four-bedroomed house in Romford. If the rateable value of the house is £500 and the rate is 65p in the £, how much will Alan have to pay every half year?
3 Mrs Lorna Milford occupies a three-bedroomed house in Newcastle. If the rateable value is £380 and the rate is 72p in the £, how much will she have to pay every year to the local authority for rates?
4 Mrs Renata Vincetti owns a restaurant in West Ham. It has been assessed at £950 for rating purposes, and the local authority have fixed the rate at 79p in the £ for the current year. How much will the quarterly bill for rates amount to?

Group task

Working together try to draw up a list of the uses to which monies such as these are put by the local authorities.

A further task

Sally shares a flat in Kensington with her friends Rachel and Ursula. They each pay one-third of the bills. Sally wants to buy a new dress she has seen but is wondering whether she can afford it. It is half-way through the month and she has £56.75 of her pay cheque left. She expects £16 of this to go on fares and food for the rest of the month, but there are also some other bills to meet. Unfortunately Ursula has gone home to Ipswich for the weekend – with the bills in her bag, so Sally has got to do some detective work to find how much the bills are for.

She knows they have used 1138 units of electricity, and that the charge is 2.613p per unit. To this has to be added the standing quarterly charge of £3.15.

The gas bill is a little more complicated. There is a standing quarterly charge of £2.75. The first 52 therms (i.e. units of gas) are charged at 22.8p per therm. Any additional therms consumed are charged at 15.3p per therm. Sally knows they have consumed about 115 therms during the three months covered by the bill.

It is a lovely dress, but it costs £26.75. Sally has to make up her mind. Can she afford the dress? What advice would you give her?

The rent for the flat is paid monthly in advance – on the first day of the month – and Sally receives her pay cheque on the last day of the month.

Questions for discussion by the group

1 Why do you think the Gas Board offers a tariff like this?
2 What can be said in its favour, and what can be said against it?

24 THE SALES REPRESENTATIVES

Sheila Armitage is the first female sales representative ever appointed by Southern Bakeries Ltd, so the Sales Manager is naturally very interested to find out how effective she is. She joined the company just over six months ago at about the same time as two young men, Adrian Phillips and Eddie Marshall, who are of a similar age to Sheila. After a short spell of training the three young representatives were allocated to their respective sales areas. The areas are of broadly similar type and the numbers of customers on the books at the start of their operations are shown below in parentheses:

Adrian was allocated the Basingstoke area (636)
Eddie was allocated the Winchester area (595)
Sheila was allocated the Eastleigh area (622)

The sales they achieved in the first six months are shown in Figure 2.8. Do you think Sheila's record compares favourably or unfavourably with her male counterparts? What comments would you make about the three performances at this stage?

Using the graph as your source of data, and rounding the sales to the nearest £100, complete the following table showing the sales staff's record during the period under review:

	June	July	Aug	Sep	Oct	Nov	Total
Adrian							
Eddie							
Sheila							
Total							

Now use this information to draw your own graphs showing the monthly cumulative sales for Eddie and Sheila. Adrian's cumulative monthly totals have already been plotted as a guide for you (see Figure 2.9).

Some further calculations for you

1 Sheila's sales of pastries for the past month were 34% of the total sales of these items. If her sales of pastries amounted to £376.80, what were the total sales?*

---

*Make your calculations on the following lines:

If 34% of sales of pastries = £376.80
1% ,, ,, ,, ,, = ?
and 100% ,, ,, ,, ,, = ?

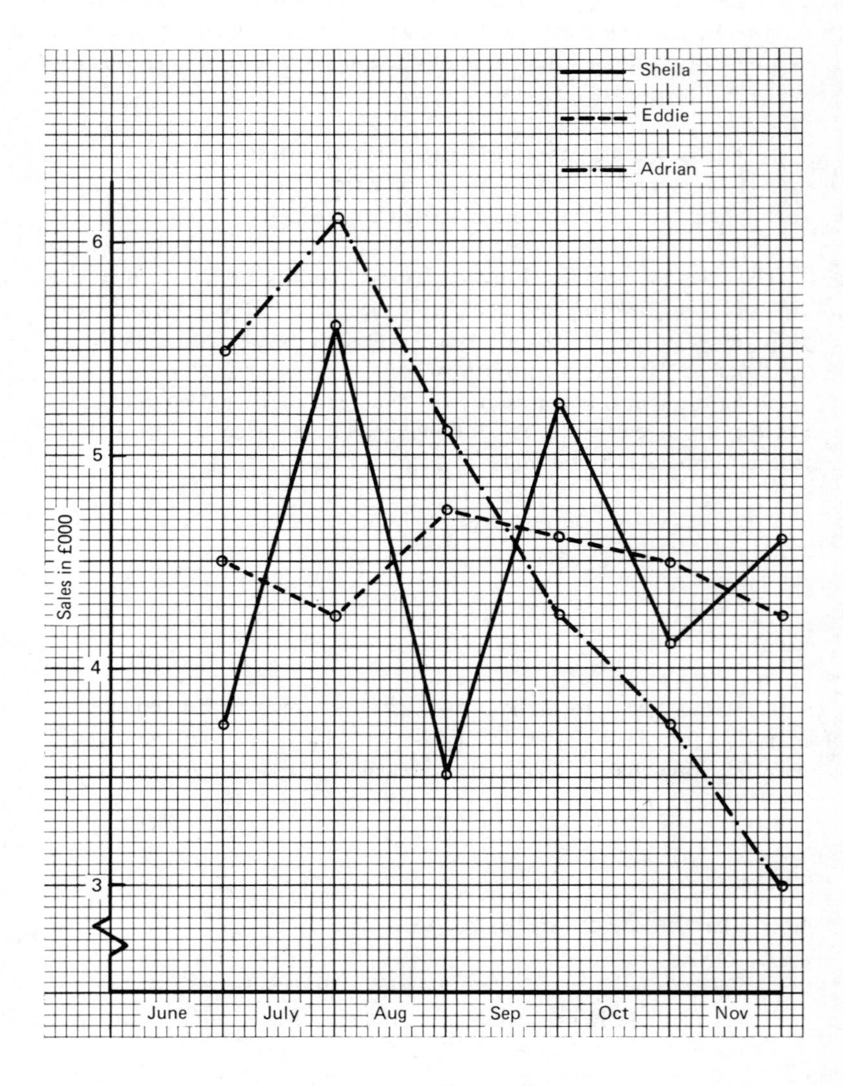

FIGURE 2.8 *Sales at Southern Bakeries Ltd. Selected Staff*

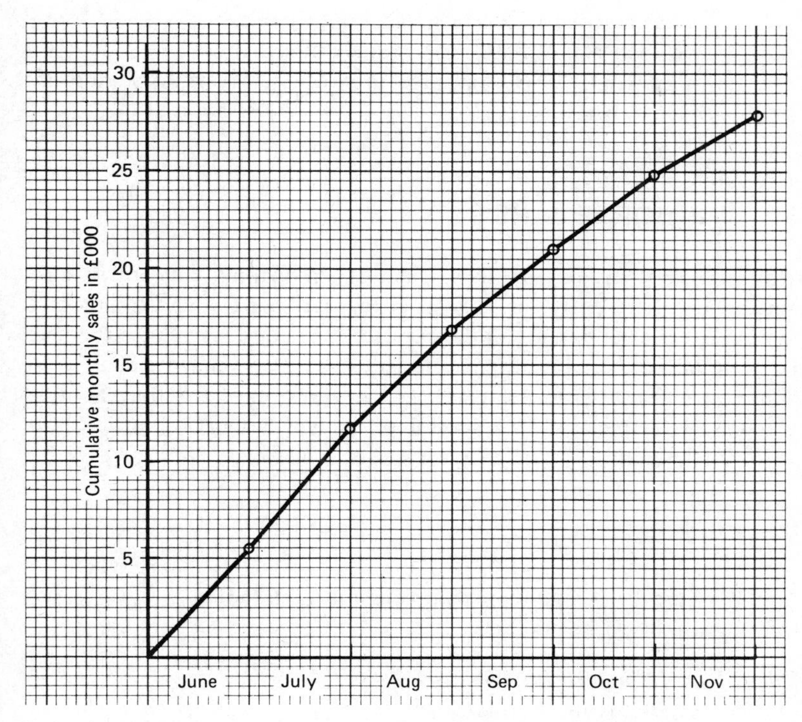

FIGURE 2.9 *Cumulative Sales of Selected Staff*

2 Sheila has used an average of 62 litres of petrol a week on her visits to customers. If this was 85% of what her predecessor used on similar visits, what was his weekly consumption of petrol?

Questions for the group

1 Which of the graphs gives the best indication of the trio's performances to date?
2 What factors other than ability might account for the differences in the results of the three sales representatives?
3 Would your assessment of the trio's performances change if you were told that their predecessors had achieved the following levels of sales in the six months leading up to June?

Basingstoke £4700 (average monthly sales)
Winchester £23500 (total for six months)
Eastleigh £3900 (average monthly sales for four months only)

25 JAMBOREE JARS LTD

This company makes jars for a famous jam-making concern in East Anglia. It has recently introduced a new jar shape which is aimed at making it easier to extract all the jam from the container. Since the new jar is squatter than the original design, it has been called a 'Flatty' – and you will see from the graph of sales over the past four months (Figure 2.10) (since the introduction of the new design) – Flatties seem to be catching on.

Your first task

Study Figure 2.10 and then complete the table below it, taking the information from the graph:

Sales of jars (March to June inclusive)

	Standards	Flatties
March		
April		
May		
June		

Your second tasks

1 By referring to the graph predict the sales for July and August, both for the Standard containers and the new Flatties. Be as accurate as you can.
2 If the Standard design was fetching 85p per dozen for Jamboree Jars, and the new Flatties were fetching 95p per dozen for them, how much would the company have received from the sale of jars between March and June inclusive? When you have completed this part of the exercise compare your answers with the other members of the group.

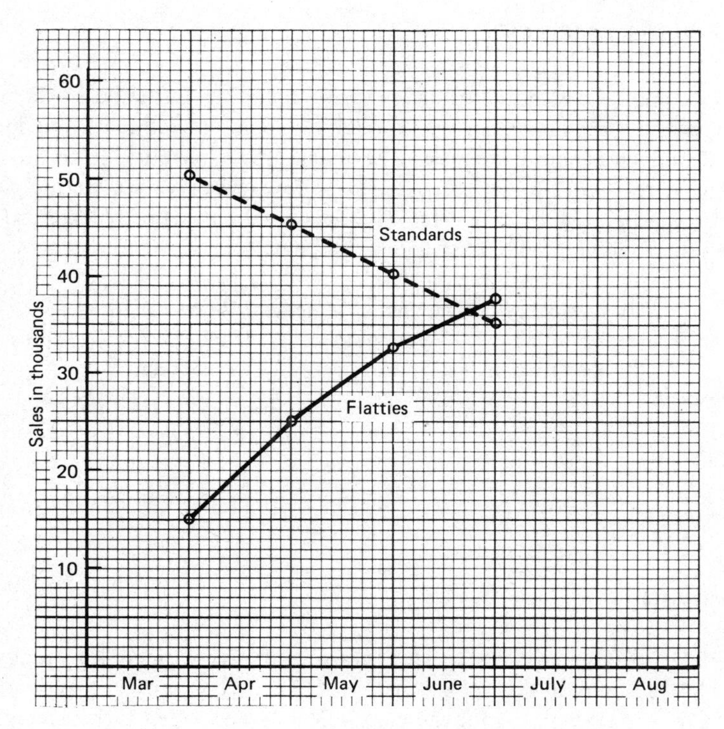

FIGURE 2.10

Your third task

On a particular day 73 Flatties were rejected by the Inspector because of faults he found in them. If these faulty Flatties represented 4.8% of the total output of Flatties on that day, how many were turned out?

For group discussion

1. At present Jamboree Jars are geared to produce 40000 Standard Jars and 40000 Flatties per month. To what extent would you change the production levels in the light of recent sales?
2. Do you think the executives at Jamboree Jars should be satisfied with the figures shown here?
3. What does 'Ltd' (Limited) mean in the firm's name?

26 ALPHA MOTORS

This is a small car-manufacturing company operating on the outskirts of Liverpool. It produces a single model of sports car which is highly priced and sells mainly overseas. The management have begun to look closely at the work-force because orders for new cars have started to decline in the past few months. The Personnel Department have produced the following table for the management:

Workers classified according to age and department

Age range	Spraying Department	Production Line	Inspection Department	Stores
Under 21	37	62	6	8
21–35	29	248	20	22
36–50	18	318	36	26
over 50	5	87	4	11

Questions

1. If 19% of the workers under the age of 36 are women, how many men are there in this age group?
2. If the total wages bill for the year is £4,324,865, what is the average annual wage?
3. What percentage of the workers are on the Production Line?

Your next task

Study the graph that follows (see Figure 2.11). It has been prepared by Alpha's Personnel Department. Working in small groups you are asked to prepare a list of ten statements about the work-force at Alpha Motors on the evidence you have here. For example:

(i) the majority of workers in the Spraying Department are under the age of 36; and
(ii) the proportion of females in the work-force increased between 1974 and 1978.

When you have completed your lists compare them with those of the other groups. Can you agree on the statements?

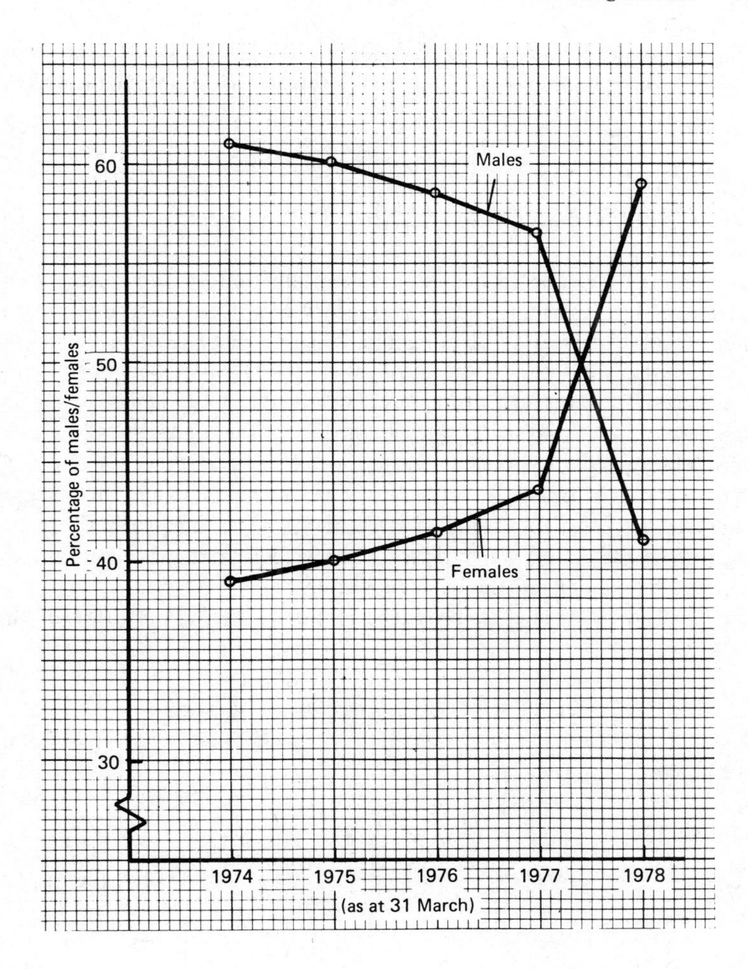

FIGURE 2.11 *Proportion of Males/Females: Alpha Motors*

Your final tasks

1 You are asked to estimate the average age of the work-force on the evidence available here. Discuss the problem together and decide how to go about it. When you have agreed on a method work out the answers separately, but compare your results at the end of the exercise.

2 Assuming the ratio between males and females now is the same as it was on 31 March 1978, how many females are employed by Alpha Motors?

27 CHRISTMAS CRACKERS

Pennington Novelties Ltd make crackers and indoor fireworks, essentially for the Christmas trade. The factory is a fairly small one – situated on the outskirts of Birmingham. The company used to be run by Percy Phipps who started the business – virtually in his own back yard – some fifty years ago. But Percy has retired and handed over the business to his grandson, Darren. Although the business has grown considerably over the years, Darren would like to see it expanding further. He has joined forces with the company's accountant, Charles Grieves, who has been involved with the business for nearly 30 years, to produce the following statistics. Darren feels that these figures may help him to understand the business better.

One of the tables they produced relates to the composition of the work-force:

TABLE 1 *Work-force by age and sex*

	Men	Women	Total
Age under 21	5	25	30
„ 21–40	11	33	44
„ over 40	59	96	155
Total	75	154	229

Another of the tables they produced related to wages:

TABLE 2 *Weekly pay packets (gross) for week ending last Friday*

	Men	Women	Total
from £25 to £34.99	3	4	7
" £35 to £44.99	11	56	67
" £45 to £54.99	24	76	100
" £55 to £64.99	19	18	37
" £65 to £74.99	18	0	18

A final table relates to the annual sales of their products over the past three years:

TABLE 3 *Sales over past three years (in £000)*

	3 years ago	2 years ago	Last year
Crackers	894	912	945
Indoor fireworks	172	168	162
Other novelties	31	64	84
Total	1097	1144	1191
Home	not available	875	946
Overseas	not available	269	245

Questions

1 What are the average earnings of the male workers? (You will have to *assume* that the three males earning between £25 and £34.99 per week are earning the mid-point in the range, i.e. £30 per week, and likewise for the other groups.)

2 What are the average earnings of the female workers?

3 What is the percentage increase in last year's sales compared with the previous year's sales?

4 Calculate the sales per worker last year, using the first and third tables above.

Your next tasks

1 Produce a bar chart, pie chart or similar diagram to illustrate the information contained in any one of the tables here. When this has been done, compare the results and decide together which presentation was most effective.

2 Working in twos and threes draw up a list of ten statements you can make about the statistics shown here for Pennington Novelties Ltd, in the same manner as in the previous assignment.

Questions for group discussion

1 Would you be satisfied with the sales figures if you were Darren Phipps? What advice would you give him?
2 Why do you think the women at Pennington Novelties – as elsewhere – earn generally less than the men?
3 Do you think people who have worked a long time for a company should be paid more than those who have recently joined, or do you think people should be paid for the job they are doing regardless of how long they have been doing it?

28 WALLS & DAWS (ESTATE AGENTS)

Andy Evans works in an estate agents office, and has just completed a rather successful month. Although he is not yet 20 years of age, he has negotiated the sale of five different properties. He is now preparing the bills which will be required for the collection of the agents' fees. Walls & Daws charge fees in accordance with the accompanying schedule:

For properties under £12500
5½% on the first £5000 of the selling price
3½% on the remainder

For properties between £12500 and £30000
5% on the first £5000 of the selling price
3½% on the remainder

For properties of £30000 and over
3½% on the first £10000 of the selling price
2½% on the remainder

Andy has worked out the charges and has asked his secretary, Louise Frampton, to check. He may be a good salesman but his calculations leave a lot to be desired, as you can see!

1 Sale of 14 Carbury Crescent, Neasden for Mrs J. McArthur for £17500

5% of £5000	=	£250
3½% of £12500	=	£315.50
		£565.50

2 Sale of Flat 76, Cranston Court, Cranston Road, Neasden for Miss I. Leadbeater for £9500

5% of £5000	=	£250
3½% of £4500	=	£157.50
		£425.50

3 Sale of Churchill Grange, Bonniface Drive, Neasden for Mr and Mrs W. Carver for £37500

3½% of £10000	=	£350
2½% of £27000	=	£675
		£1025.00

What mistakes would Louise have found? And how much would the mistakes have cost the firm if they had not been corrected?

Perhaps wisely, Andy let Louise make out the last two accounts on her own:

4 Flat 4A, Gordon Rise, Park Lane, Neasden was sold for Mr Maurice Stranks for £22475

5 165 Fernvale Drive, Neasden was sold for Mr and Mrs L. Dugdale for £32750

How would she have made out the accounts?

Andy is entitled to a personal commission on the sales. The commission is added to his monthly pay cheque and is based on the following scale:

½% on the first £10000 of the price
¼% on the next £10000 of the price
⅛% on the remainder

How much commission would he receive from the sale of the five properties – after tax had been deducted at 34p in the £?

A group task

Study the local press and produce a collective report on the price ranges of properties in your area. Distinguish between newly constructed houses and flats and those which are being sold by the occupiers.

Questions for the group to discuss

1 What are the advantages and disadvantages of being paid according to results as Andy is?
2 Why do you think Walls & Daws have these particular schedules for their fees? Is it to attract owners of the lower-priced properties? What sort of justification is there for this differential treatment?
3 What services do the estate agents render to their clients, and how are their fees justified?

29 SEASONAL DEMANDS

When Julius Kringle started his ice-cream business shortly after the Second World War it seemed unlikely that it would succeed. There seemed to be too much competition for one thing, and Julius seemed to be permanently short of cash for another. But Julius concentrated on selling economically priced extra large cartons to hotels and guest houses in his native Bournemouth – and with the backing of a sympathetic bank manager overcame the early difficulties. He ploughed back the bulk of his profits into the business and it eventually flourished. He now has a host of regular customers along the whole of the South Coast.

There was another problem that Julius had to face. The demand for his ice-cream was very seasonal. So he looked around for another product which would have a demand pattern which was exactly opposite to the demand for ice-cream. Ice-cream sales peak in the summer, and Julius wanted a product which would have peak sales in winter. And he found it! He started manufacturing powdered soups. The basic ingredient was the same for both his ice-cream and his soup – dried milk. The customers were also the same. His vans delivered ice-cream mix and/or soup powder to the hoteliers as they required. Whenever orders for ice-cream fell, almost invariably orders for soup increased. Initially sales still peaked in the holiday season, but Julius has recently begun to sell quantities of his soup powders to one of the large food-retailing chains.

The seasonal nature of the demand for Julius Kringle's ice-cream and soup powders is shown in the bar charts featured in Figures 2.12 and 2.13.

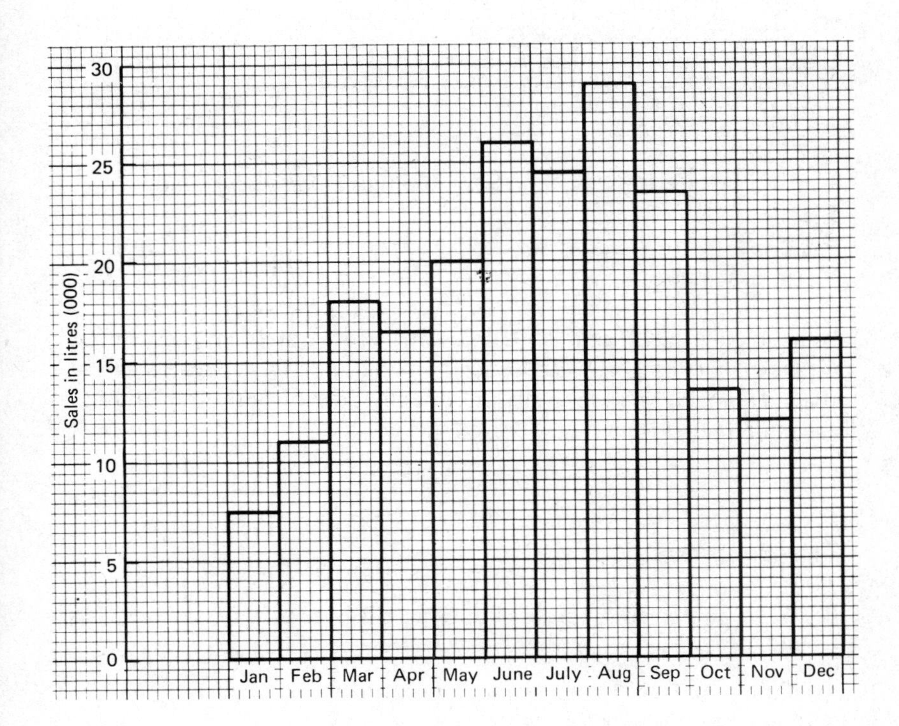

FIGURE 2.12 *Sales of Ice-Cream in litres (000)*

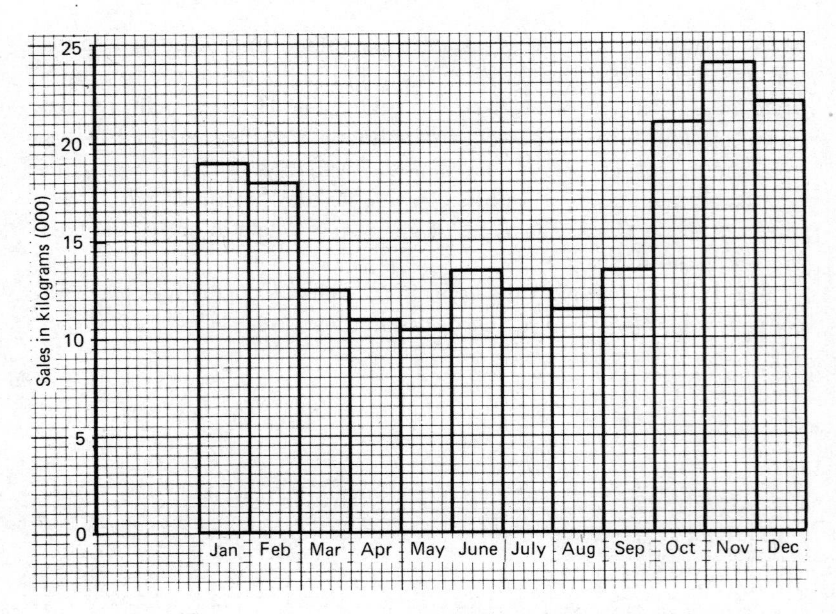

FIGURE 2.13 *Sales of Soups in kilograms (000)*

Your first task

Using Figures 2.12 and 2.13, calculate as accurately as possible the total sales of ice-cream and soup for the 12-month period. Using the statistics you now have available, plot the sales of both soup and ice-cream on the graph in Figure 2.14

The group task

Break up into small groups and draw up a list of as many statements as possible regarding the statistics shown here. For example:

(i) More soup is sold in the winter months than the summer.
(ii) January is the worst month for ice-cream sales.

Which team has produced the longest list?

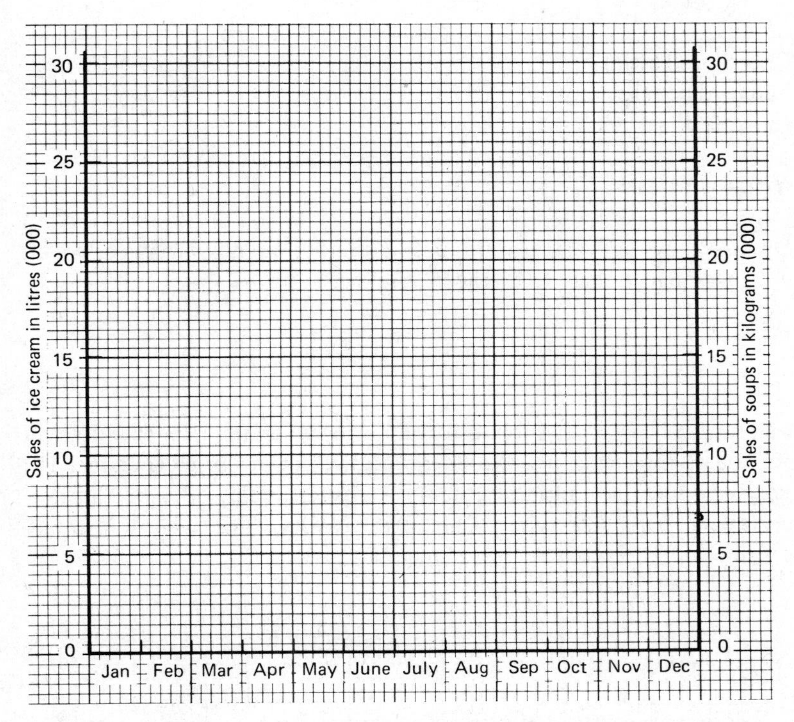

FIGURE 2.14 *Sales of Soups and Ice-Cream in kilograms and litres (000)*

30 CHOCOLATE BARS

A famous chocolate manufacturer has introduced some new novelty bars on to the market. There are three different bars, namely:

(i) Chocolate Tasties – raisins in ginger biscuit covered with plain chocolate
(ii) Tender Thoughts – fudge and caramel in milk chocolate
(iii) Chocolate Lingers – nougat and biscuit centres in plain chocolate

The manufacturer is charging the same price for each of the bars, and some market research has been conducted on 1000 schoolchildren. They were asked their preference when given small free samples of each of the bars. The results are shown over:

	1st Choice	2nd Choice	3rd Choice
Chocolate Tasties	364	574	62
Tender Thoughts	217	118	665
Chocolate Lingers	419	308	273

Your first task

Discuss these results as a group and decide, on this evidence, which chocolate bar is likely to be the best seller.

Your second task

Figures 2.15 and 2.16 show what happened when the firm produced all three bars for a trial period. When you look at the graph (Figure 2.15) you will see that during September, for example, 50% of the new chocolate bars sold were Chocolate Tasties, 40% were Chocolate Lingers and 10% were Tender Thoughts.

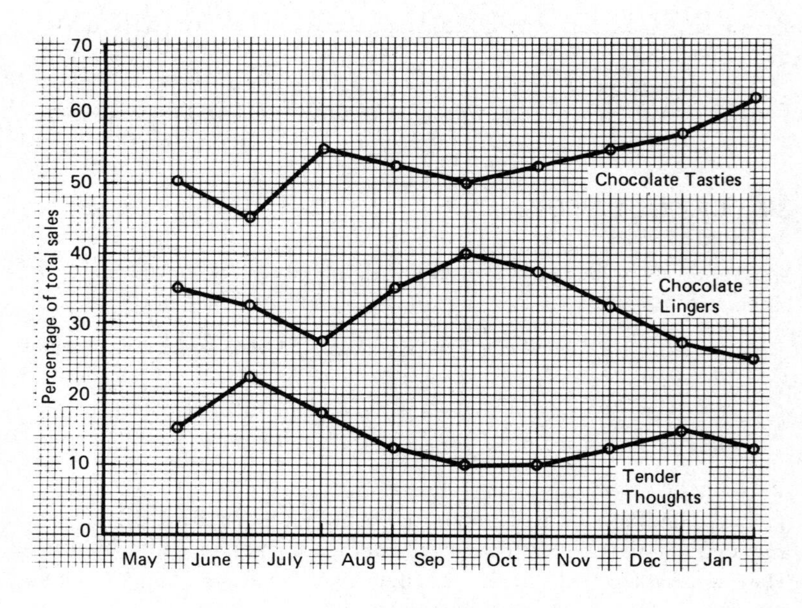

FIGURE 2.15 *Sales of New Chocolate Bars*

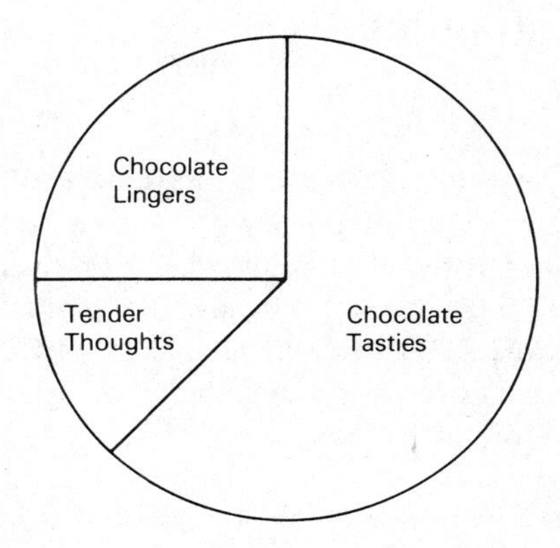

FIGURE 2.16

Relate the pie chart shown in Figure 2.16 to the graph. Can you tell which month this chart relates to?

Your third task

Complete the following table, using the percentages given in the graph to calculate the missing figures:

	Chocolate Tasties	Chocolate Lingers	Tender Thoughts	Total (in 000)
May				300
June				304
July				308
August				309
September				318
October				323
November				341
December				351
January				362
Total				2916

Note: The method required is shown by the following example:
Chocolate Tasties accounted for 45% of sales in June (according to the graph)
Total sales in June were 304000 (according to the table)
45% of 304,000 = 136800 (137000 to the nearest 1000)
So 137 goes into the appropriate column.

31 ORION INSURANCE

Part 1

The company in question operates a fire-insurance policy which covers properties against loss or destruction by fire. Premiums are calculated in the following manner. If the cover required is £10000 and the company require £1 for every £100 of cover they give, the premium will be 1% of £10000, which equals £100 (payable annually). In fact the premiums required from the policy-holders under the Orion scheme vary according to the classifications indicated:

65p per £100 cover on private property (Class A)
85p per £100 cover on shops and offices (Class B)
95p per £100 cover on industrial premises (Class C)

You are asked to calculate the annual premium required from the following policy-holders:

		Cover (£)	Premium (£)
Grimm's Chemists, High Street, Cheam	B	10000	
Westchester Bank, Leamington Spa	B	12750	
John Gray, 45 Gunn Street, Oldham	A	7500	
A.P. Hobbs Ltd, Bolden Road, Barnsley	C	30000	
J.C. Cramner, Minns Close, Huddersfield	A	12500	
Denzel Glass, Salisbury	C	25500	
A. Goldthorpe, 15 Aldis Drive, Hove	A	22500	
Industrial Products Ltd, Swindon	C	125000	
Mrs R. Gibbs, 33 Dean Crescent, Stoke	A	6250	
Fenner Fashions, High Street, Norwich	B	32000	
The Tuck Box, Station Approach, Rugby	B	12000	
Benham Woodyard, Lever Street, Liverpool	C	42500	
	Total		£

Part 2

Mark Christopher's Motor Mart Ltd have insurance cover with the Orion and they recently suffered extensive damage as a result of a fire in their showrooms. The claim for the damage to the premises is being dealt with separately, but under consideration at this time is the stock of second-hand cars which were completely destroyed.

	Asking prices (£)
1975 Chrysler 180	1500
1975 Toyota Celica 1600	2000
1976 Ford Cortina 2000	2395
1976 Triumph Dolomite 1500	2195
1976 Peugeot 504 Estate	3475
1976 Range Rover	6250
1977 Ford Escort 1.3	2525
1977 MGB Roadster	2849
1978 Ford Escort 1.3	2865
1978 Citroen CX 2400	4850

Orion have agreed to pay compensation to the Motor Mart to the extent of 65% of the asking prices shown. How much would that amount to?

Part 3

Orion also offer marine insurance cover. The oil tanker *Persian Prince* was insured for a total of £3,300,000. The insurance was arranged by a syndicate which has divided the policy into 1500 parts or shares of which Orion have been allocated 72 such shares. Unfortunately the *Persian Prince* has been lost at sea and the insurance syndicate is required to meet the claim by the owners. How much will Orion's proportion of the claim be?

Questions for the group to discuss

1. Why do you think the insurance company only paid out 65% of the asking price for the cars which were destroyed?
2. Why do you think the *Persian Prince* insurance was arranged through a syndicate rather than a single insurance firm?
3. If insurance companies take on other people's risks, how is it they are generally so profitable and safe?

32 CRAMPTON ELECTRICS

When Tony Crampton left school he went to work for the local Electricity Board as an apprentice electrician, but when he married Abigail she encouraged him to go into business on his own account. It worked out quite well, because Abigail's widowed mother provided the couple with the necessary funds, and Abigail was able to keep the books and run the shop while Tony concentrated on the technical side. They concentrated their attention on rewiring worn-out electrical installations in old houses and installing electrical systems in new ones. Tony was able to develop profitable contacts with a firm of builders, and as they flourished so did he.

Tony now has a total of 15 skilled electricians working for him and they have been very busy over the past two months getting a high-rise block of flats ready for occupation. As a result of the pressure of work, Tony's work-force has been getting a fair amount of overtime pay. Abigail is in charge of this and she has prepared a list of the staff and the amount of overtime they earned last week. The electricians have been graded in three broad classifications according to their qualifications and experience:

A is the top grade and carries overtime at £2.64 per hour
B is the middle grade and carries overtime at £2.46 per hour
C is the lowest grade and carries overtime at £2.16 per hour

Abigail looks at the overtime list in front of her:

Name	Overtime hours	Grade	Overtime pay (£)
Acres, J.	3 hrs 20 mins	B	8.20
White, T.W.	2 hrs 30 mins	A	6.60
Abercrombie, P.	4 hrs	B	10.56
Patel, A.	3 hrs 25 mins	B	8.41
Lever, S.	7 hrs 5 mins	C	15.54
Sharami, B.	2 hrs 45 mins	A	7.26
Jones, K.	4 hrs 35 mins	B	11.28
White, P.W.	3 hrs	C	6.48
Tomlinson, D.	2 hrs 55 mins	B	7.18
McGuire, A.	5 hrs 10 mins	A	13.64
Judd, K.	1 hr 30 mins	B	3.69
Crispin, T.	3 hrs 50 mins	C	8.28
Palmerston, L.	4 hrs 30 mins	B	11.07
Anderson, M.	2 hrs 15 mins	B	4.86
Spiegel, J.	5 hrs 5 mins	A	13.42
	Total overtime pay		£136.47

Abigail looks at the total time which is shown on the work-sheets and realises the pay about to be credited is more than it should be:

Work-sheet totals

Hours worked	Grade	Total
15 hrs 30 mins	A	£40.92
26 hrs 30 mins	B	£65.21
13 hrs 55 mins	C	£30.06
		£136.19

Your task

1 You are asked to correct the calculations for Abigail so that each employee is credited with only the overtime to which he is entitled.

2 Income tax has to be deducted before overtime can be paid. Everyone other than T.W. White has tax deducted at 34p in the £. White is taxed on one-third of his overtime at 25p in the £, the remainder being taxed at 34p in the £. Show the amount of cash actually received for overtime work, i.e. after the deduction of tax.

Supplementary questions

3 Calculate the average amount of gross overtime (*arithmetic mean*) earned by Tony Crampton's employees during the week.

4 Which pay grade is the *mode*?

5 Which is the *median* overtime pay?

Questions for discussion by the group

1 Do you think people should get the *same rate* of pay for overtime as for normal work, or should overtime attract a *higher rate*? Why? How do you think the *rate* of overtime pay should be determined? Relate your arguments to any specific jobs with which you are familiar.

2 What effect do you think a high rate of tax has on people's willingness to earn? Who would suffer if the rate of tax were to be lowered?

3 Would it be possible to prepare a Ready Reckoner for each of the three rates over the range required so as to help Abigail in the future? How would you go about doing it?

33 AMATEUR DRAMATICS

Susan Slade is hoping to become a professional actress one day. At the moment, apart from working at Mortimer's Department Stores during the day, she is involved in the local Amateur Dramatic Society and finds herself doing all sorts of things to keep it going. Their latest effort was to put on a single Sunday-night performance of a new farce entitled *The Secretaries' Secret*. Written by one of the Society's own members, it has attracted a lot of publicity in the local press. The play was staged in the Phoenix Theatre in the town centre.

Apart from playing a small part herself Susan has been made responsible for the finances in connection with the venture. She is now beginning to collect the information required to decide whether *The Secretaries' Secret* was a financial success or not.

The following information is available.

Cash proceeds from sales by attendants (volunteers from the society)

Ice-cream	£15.89	
Sweets	£10.12	
Soft drinks	£12.35	

Invoices received (already paid)

Phoenix Theatre: Hire of theatre		£105.00
Hire of trays, etc.		£ 2.20
		£107.20

The *Evening Echo*: advertisements 3 x £5.60

Invoices received but not yet paid

Stanford Printers: Posters	£ 18.55
Programmes	£ 11.65
De Groote Theatrical Costumiers:	
Costumes for *Fanny by Gaslight*	£ 38.95
Costumes for *The Secretaries' Secret*	£ 9.95
	£ 48.90

Fanshaw's Candy Bar:	Ice-cream	£ 16.00
	Sweets	£ 8.50
	Iced drinks	£ 12.00
		£ 36.50
	less 12½% discount	

(*Note:* Gordon Fanshaw is a member of the Society and has agreed to allow a special discount of 12½% on the sundries purchased through him. He has also agreed to take back unsold items. These totalled £1.15 only (all sweets).)

All the tickets were sold through an agency in town, and although they have not been able to produce an account for Susan yet, it has provided a chart (see Figure 2.17) which shows the seats that were sold. She has been told the agency's account will be made up from this chart in due course. It will take 15% commission on all sales – as was arranged.

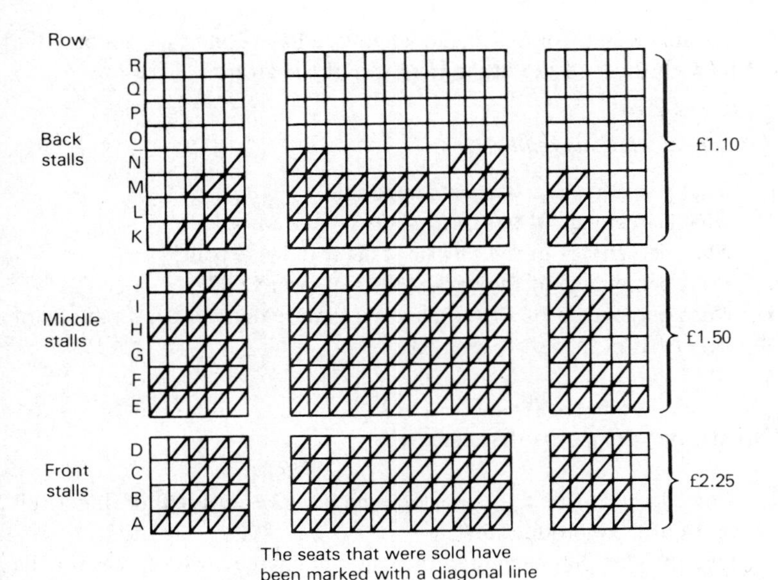

FIGURE 2.17 *The Phoenix Theatre – Sunday . . . . . .*

The Society's Treasurer has asked Susan to prepare a simple account showing the sums paid out and the sums received in relation to *The Secretaries' Secret*. He produces the account that was prepared from the previous production – *Fanny by Gaslight* – and asks her to use the same style of presentation.

Receipts and payments account for 'Fanny by Gaslight' (14–16 June)

Expenditure		(£)	Income	(£)
Costumes	32.89		Receipts from sale	
add bill outstanding	38.95	71.84	of tickets	296.69
Advertising expenses		14.50	Profit from sale	
Hire of theatre		205.00	of refreshments	24.65
Sundries		17.50		
Profit c/d		12.50		
		£321.34		£321.34
			Profit b/d	12.50

Your task

Prepare an account for Susan and when you have done this compare the results with those of the other members of the group.

Further calculations required

1. What percentage of the seats were sold?
2. What percentage of the front stalls seats were sold?
3. What percentage of the middle stalls seats were sold?
4. What percentage of the back stalls seats were sold?
5. What percentage of the total receipts were derived from the sale of tickets from the latest production?

Questions for group discussion

1. How do you think the Society might have ensured getting a full house for the production?
2. One member has suggested they should charge higher prices for the food and drinks at the next show, while another member has suggested reducing the prices. Which view do you favour, and why?

3 Do you think there would be any advantages in offering all the seats at the same price?
4 What are the arguments for and against using the services of a ticket agency? What are the alternatives?

34 WEDDING BELLS

Paul and Joanne were planning to marry. They both worked at Benton's Department Store in London's West End. Paul was an Assistant Buyer in the Furniture Department, while Joanne was a Sales Assistant in the Shoe Department. Joanne's father did not really approve of Paul, but agreed to give his blessing as long as the couple were able to save £1000. Paul had £270 to start with and Joanne had saved £140 from her salary. On 31 December they paid these sums into an account in their joint names at the local Trustee Savings Bank.

Benton's Store were paying Paul a commission of 5% on all sales over £600 in any calendar month and he agreed to pay all his commission into the account, ignoring any tax that might be deducted from his pay cheque relating to the commission. For the following 12 months Paul's sales were as shown below. Your first task is to complete the details by adding the missing figures in the three end columns.

Paul's sales and commission for the year

	Sales for the month (£)	Excess over £600	Commission for month	Running total of commission
Jan	1525.30	£925.30	£46.25	£46.25
Feb	1106.20	£506.20	£25.31	£71.56
Mar	2811.25			
Apr	2296.76			
May	2495.80			
June	1108.30			
July	1326.60			
Aug	1722.35			
Sep	1235.17			
Oct	1000.40			
Nov	804.80			
Dec	1868.65			

Questions

1 At the end of which month would the couple have reached their target of £1000, assuming no sums were withdrawn and the only payments into the account were those representing Paul's commission?

2 What was the average balance on the Trustee Savings account throughout the year? Bearing in mind this figure, how much interest could Paul and Joanne have expected to be credited to their joint account at the end of the year if the rate of interest allowed by the Trustee Savings Bank was 7½% per annum?

After the wedding Joanne decided to keep a careful record of their income and expenses. She did this for the first three months and the incomplete details are shown below. Can you complete the accounts for her? The missing figures need to be written in at (a), (b), (c), (d) and (e).

April's account

		(£)		(£)
Rent and rates		60.00	Balance at the start of April	322.75
Coal		22.24		
Hire-purchase payments			Paul's pay cheque for month	165.35
Furniture	32.00			
Carpets	21.25	53.25	Joanne's pay cheque for month	134.63
Housekeeping		100.00		
New clothes		35.25		
Television rental		25.00		
Fares		15.25		
Pocket money		40.00		
Balance at end of April		(a)		
		£622.73		£622.73

May's account

	(£)		(£)
Rent and rates	48.00	Balance at the start of May	(a)
Hire-purchase payments		Paul's pay for month	160.65
Furniture 32.00		Joanne's pay for month	134.63
Carpets 21.25	53.25		
Television rental	20.00		
Fares	14.75		
Housekeeping	80.00		
Pocket money	32.00		
Balance at end of May	______ (b)		______
	______ (c)		______ (c)

June's account

	(£)		(£)
Rent and rates	60.00	Balance at the start of June	(b)
Hire-purchase payments		Paul's pay for month	175.32
Furniture 32.00		Joanne's pay for month	139.80
Carpets 21.25	53.25		
Television rental	20.00		
Fares	14.75		
Housekeeping	80.00		
Pocket money	32.00		
Balance at end of June	______ (d)		______
	______ (e)		______ (e)
		Balance at the start of July	______ (d)

Some questions for the group to consider

1 What comments can you make about Joanne's accounts?
2 Are Joanne and Paul saving much?
3 Are they in any sort of financial difficulty?
4 What advice would you offer them (on the evidence here)?
5 Do you think it is better to save up for something rather than to buy it on hire-purchase?

6 What items, other than those included here, might you have expected to find in Joanne's informal accounts?

7 What alternatives are there to keeping the money in a Trustee Savings Bank account? What are the merits and demerits of the alternatives?

35 SAM'S PLACE

After leaving school Samantha Wright tried a number of different jobs but failed to settle down in any one of them. One of her friends had opened a boutique in Wolverhampton and the more she heard about this venture, the more she was tempted to do the same sort of thing herself. Her friend suggested the name for the new shop – 'Sam's Place' – and Samantha was completely sold on the idea from that moment on. She contacted a firm that manufactured denims and they offered her such favourable terms that she decided to concentrate on their products exclusively. What pleased her most was that everyone was prepared to give her credit. The denim manufacturers were prepared to give her three months before requiring payment. The shop-owner required only one month's rent in advance (the rent and rates came to £72 per calendar month). The bank gave Samantha a loan of £200 which Samantha used together with her own stake of £200 cash to fit out the conveniently sited little shop as attractively as possible.

Her younger sister helped out on Saturdays. Otherwise Samantha managed on her own, even though it was sometimes hectic. As her bills seemed to relate to calendar months or quarters, Samantha paid her sister in the same way – £25 per calendar month. She paid over a cheque on the first day of each month.

Soon after she opened Sam's Place Samantha met a young trainee accountant, Andy Brightwell. Andy not only took Samantha seriously, he took his job, and her business, seriously. She knew that the business was doing quite well. She had drawn out £300 for personal spending and there was still plenty of money going into her account. But Andy suggested she should find out how much profit she had made, not only gross profit, but net profit too. Samantha thought he was trying to blind her with science, but he explained that one needs to know not only the gross profit that one has made – that is, the difference between the cost of articles sold and the cash one has received for them – but the net profit, i.e. the gross profit less all costs incurred in selling them, such as the rent of the shop, the cost of heating and lighting, her sister's wages, and so on.

As Andy explained, it is dangerous to start spending profits until you know exactly where you stand.

'It should be easy to find out,' he said. 'You started on New Year's Day. It's the 31 March today. Let's find out – now!'

With an air of masculine superiority Andy set about elaborating the technique for her. He drew up the following skeleton account for her and said all she would have to do was complete the figures.

'This is the way accountants do it,' he said proudly.

Trading and profit and loss account for January to March

	(£)		(£)
Denims purchased (cost)		Cash received from	
less Stock unsold (cost)	______	sales of denims	
Gross profit c/d (balance)	______		______
	______		______
Rent and rates		Gross profit b/d	
Wages			
Bank charges			
Electricity			
Net profit c/d (balance)	______		______
	______		______
		Net profit b/d	

Samantha has the following information available to complete the account:

(i) The outstanding electricity bill for the quarter amounts to £74.34;

(ii) the bank charges for the quarter amount to £15.15;

(iii) there are three outstanding invoices from the denim manufacturers

	Grade	
January invoice:	A	180 garments at £4.80 each
	B	60 garments at £3.95 each
	C	72 garments at £3.75 each
February invoice:	A	120 garments at £4.80 each
	B	24 garments at £3.95 each

March invoice: Grade A 62 garments at £4.80 each
C 60 garments at £3.75 each

(iv) The stock in hand at 31 March includes the following:

176 Grade A garments
34 Grade B garments
62 Grade C garments

(v) Samantha has three standard selling prices:
Grade A garments are sold at £6.75 each
Grade B garments are sold at £5.70 each
Grade C garments are sold at £5.25 each

Your task

Complete the trading and profit and loss account for Samantha. And then turn to the balance-sheet below, filling in the figures from the information given in the narrative.

Andy explained to Samantha that the balance-sheet shows, on one side assets which could be converted into cash, and on the liabilities side the debts which are owed. These debts include the original stake which Samantha put into the business.

Balance-sheet as at 31 March

Liabilities	(£)	Assets	(£)
Capital (original stake)		Stock in hand	
add Profit	______	Cash	20
		Balance on current (cheque) account	
less Drawings (personal spending)	______	Fittings (at cost)	
Bank loan			
Creditors	______		______
	£ ______		£ ______

Questions for group discussion

1 Do you think Samantha should be pleased with these accounts?

2 Can you see any dangers for Samantha in the situation described here?
3 What do you think are the advantages and disadvantages of having your own business, as compared with working for someone else?

36 THE LEGATEES

Edith Romsey, a widow, died last year. She was 82. In her will she left the net proceeds of her freehold house in Ilford to her sister's children – George, Pamela and Stella. George is to receive 2/5ths of the proceeds, and Pamela and Stella 3/10ths each. But Stella died some years ago leaving three children – Alan, David and Susan – who are entitled to their mother's share of the estate in equal shares themselves.

The executors have taken time to sell the house but a sale has now been completed. The property fetched £16250 but the following deductions have to be made before the proceeds can be shared out among the beneficiaries:

Legal expenses

The solicitor's fees are

2¾ % on the first £5000 of the selling price

and 1⅛ % on the remainder of the proceeds

Other legal expenses total £82.50 and also have to be deducted.

Agent's commision

This is also based on the selling price. The scale of commission is:

5% on the first £5000

2½% on the next £5000

1¼% on the remainder

What were the net proceeds of the sale of the house? How much would each of the five beneficiaries receive?

George?

Pamela?

Alan?

David?

Susan?

The remainder of Edith Romsey's estate amounts to £13875.16. Her will disposes of this in the following manner:

'After payment of the following legacies
£1000 to the R.S.P.C.A.
£500 to Reverend Sydney Taylor
£30 to each of my friends, Sylvia Cheetham, Cynthia Bryant and Eleanor Fry,
thereafter the estate is to be divided into 10 parts of which
4 parts pass to Dr Barnado's Homes
3 parts pass to The Spastics Society
2 parts pass to War on Want
1 part passes to The King George's Fund for Sailors.'

How much will each of the residuary legatees (the last four charities named here) receive from Edith Romsey's will?

Susan is approaching her seventeenth birthday and has been advised to invest in National Savings Certificates. No interest is payable if the certificates are encashed within the first year, but an investment of £100 grows to £106 at the end of Year 1, £113.50 at the end of Year 2, £122.50 at the end of Year 3, and £134 at the end of Year 4. No income tax is payable.

Susan wants to know what rate of interest she will be getting from the investment. Complete the table below for her:

	Increase in value during year (£)	Average rate of interest per annum (since start)
Year 1	6.00	
Year 2	13.50	
Year 3	22.50	
Year 4	34.00	

George invested his legacy in the following Government (gilt-edged) Stocks. The solicitor explained to him that the first three stocks were called Dated Gilts because the Government would repay the stocks some time between the dates specified. The other stocks were undated and would not be repaid by the Government at any fixed date.

£1100 9% Treasury Stock 1992–6
£2600 3% British Gas Stock 1990–5
£1500 12¼% Exchequer Stock 1992
£300 2½% Consolidated Stock
£2200 3½% War Stock

George did not like the advice he received to buy some of the stocks. For example, he felt that 2½% on the Consolidated Stock was a ridiculously low rate of interest, but when he learned that he would only have to pay about £25 for every £100 of the Stock – according to the price ruling on the Stock Exchange at that time – he was much happier.

How much gross interest will George receive from these stocks?

If George has to pay tax at 42p in the £, how much net interest will he receive?

If the price of War Stock was £34.50 per £100 of stock, how much would George have had to pay for the £2200 of War Stock (ignoring brokerage charges)?
Use the following technique:

If £100 Stock costs £34.50
£1 Stock costs £(34.50/100)
and £2200 Stock costs £(34.50/100) x 2200

Questions for the group to discuss

1 How would you have advised George to invest his money – in property or in other stocks?
2 Do you think more people should be encouraged to invest in Stock Exchange securities? How do you think this could be done?

37 THE GAS BOARD

There are 15 members of staff in the office of the Gas Board at Little Embridge. They are listed below in alphabetical order with the salaries they earn alongside their names, ages and positions.

			£ per annum
Butt, Susan	(Assistant Manager)	Age 40	3872.50

Chandler, Claire	(Clerk Grade II)	Age 23	see scales
Crowther, Susan	(Clerk Grade I)	Age 19	see scales
Davidson, Peter	(Clerk Grade I)	Age 18	see scales
Gardner, Jeremy	(Manager)	Age 36	4985.00
Halpin, Alison	(Audio Typist)	Age 19	1985.25
Jardine, Colin	(Clerk Grade II)	Age 26	see scales
Langham, Sally	(Audio Typist)	Age 18	1585.00
McBride, Daniel	(Clerk Grade I)	Age 17	see scales
McNair, Liam	(Clerk Grade I)	Age 19	see scales
Oliver, Sandra	(Supervisor)	Age 51	2675.00
Parrott, Thelma	(Shorthand Typist)	Age 23	2750.00
Redmond, June	(Clerk Grade I)	Age 19	see scales
Sanderson, Elaine	(Receptionist)	Age 28	1856.50
Underwood, John	(Clerk Grade II)	Age 32	see scales

Salary scales for Clerks Grades I and II (£ per annum)

Ages	up to 18	19–22	23–26	27 and over
Grade I	1650	1775	1950	2175
Grade II	1800	2000	2200	2500

Your first tasks

1 Given the information above, you are asked to calculate the *median age* and the *average age* (*arithmetic mean*) for the staff as a whole. Also calculate the *median salary* and the *average salary* (*arithmetic mean*).
2 Now do the same calculations as above but for the female staff only.

Income tax

Of course the salaries shown on the preceding list will not be the sum received by the employee. Before the salaries are paid over the Gas Board will have to deduct an appropriate sum for income tax and national insurance. We might find, for example, that Colin Jardine has to pay about £3 a week in tax, and this would be calculated along the following lines:

		(£)	
Salary		2200	
less allowances			
Personal	1295		
Children	401		
Life insurance	15	1711	
		489	= taxable income

If the current rate of tax is 30p in the £, tax will be

30/100 x £489 = £146.70 p.a., or £2.82 per week

Your second tasks

1 Given the allowances indicated and assuming a tax rate of 25p in the £ on the first £500 of taxable income, with tax at 34p in the £ on the remainder, calculate the income tax payable by the following members of staff:

	Tax allowances
Thelma Parrott	£1505
June Redmond	£1100
Jeremy Gardner	£2550
John Underwood	£1505

2 When you have completed the tax calculations use the graph (Figure 2.18) to check your results. Can you see how the graph has been constructed?

Questions for group discussion

1 Which of the following factors ought to count most in determining whether a person is promoted to a higher grade: regular attendance and punctuality, work output, length of service, a pleasant attitude to customers, appearance?

2 Do you think it is better that pay increases are given as a matter of right, or do you think increases should be given on the basis of merit?

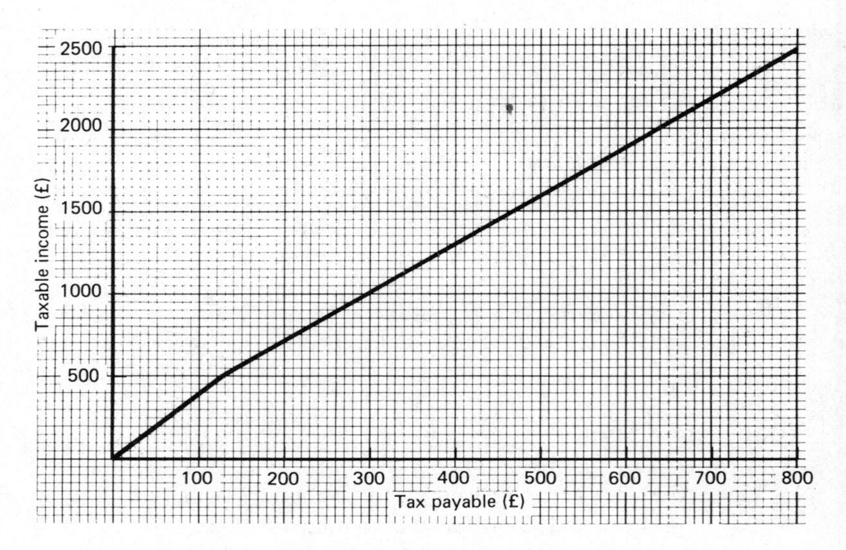

FIGURE 2.18 *Graph for calculating Tax Payable*

38 FRENCH LEAVE

Peter Phillips was delighted to be going to Nice for his holidays. His first year at work had been a hard one and he felt he had earned the break. Before he could contemplate lazing around in the sun surrounded by beautiful girls, he had to:

(i) brush up on his French;
(ii) visit his bank; and
(iii) check up on the latest exchange rates.

The bank were prepared to sell Peter French francs at the rate of 8.80 francs to the £ and he bought 600 francs to take with him while arranging a further 800 francs to be made available to him in France.

Peter had a wonderful three weeks, but he ran out of money before the end. He instructed his bank to send him a further 200 francs, but the exchange rate had changed. The new rate was 8.75 francs to the £.

When Peter arrived back in England he decided to count the cost of his holiday. In addition to the expenditure mentioned above, he had paid £216.35 to the English travel agents and £84.56 for his return air fare.

He had brought back 86 francs to England which the bank changed for him at a rate of 8.50 to the £.

How much had Peter spent altogether on his holiday?

Questions for the group

1 Were the changes in the exchange rate which occurred during the course of Peter's holiday to his advantage or detriment?
2 Why do changes in the exchange rate occur?

While Peter was in France he saw various items for sale which appealed to him. He could not remember the exact prices he would have had to pay in England for them, but he had some idea. You will see his estimate below, together with the prices which were being asked in France for the various items. You are asked to glance down the list of items and tick any 'good bargains'. Put a cross against any items which seem dearer in France. When this is done, calculate the English equivalent prices exactly – in the final column – using an exchange rate of 8.75 francs to the £. Have you changed your mind about any of the 'bargains'?

	Estimated price in England (£)	Actual price in France (francs)	Actual price equivalent (£)
Triplex electric shaver	9.00	80.50	
Apex cigarette lighter	4.15	30.75	
Red Baron sandals	7.00	60.00	
Triplex cigarette case	8.00	83.75	
Chocolate biscuits (per kilo)	2.50	15.35	
Golden Delicious apples (per kilo)	0.80	6.50	
Triplex fountain pen	10.00	70.00	
Truscan electric guitar	200.00	1650.00	
Gourmet cigars (box of 5)	1.00	7.15	
Slimtan jeans	7.50	80.00	
Snowwhite toothpaste	0.60	5.00	
Apex sunglasses	5.00	43.45	

When you have completed your calculations, study Figure 2.19 and use the graph to check your results.

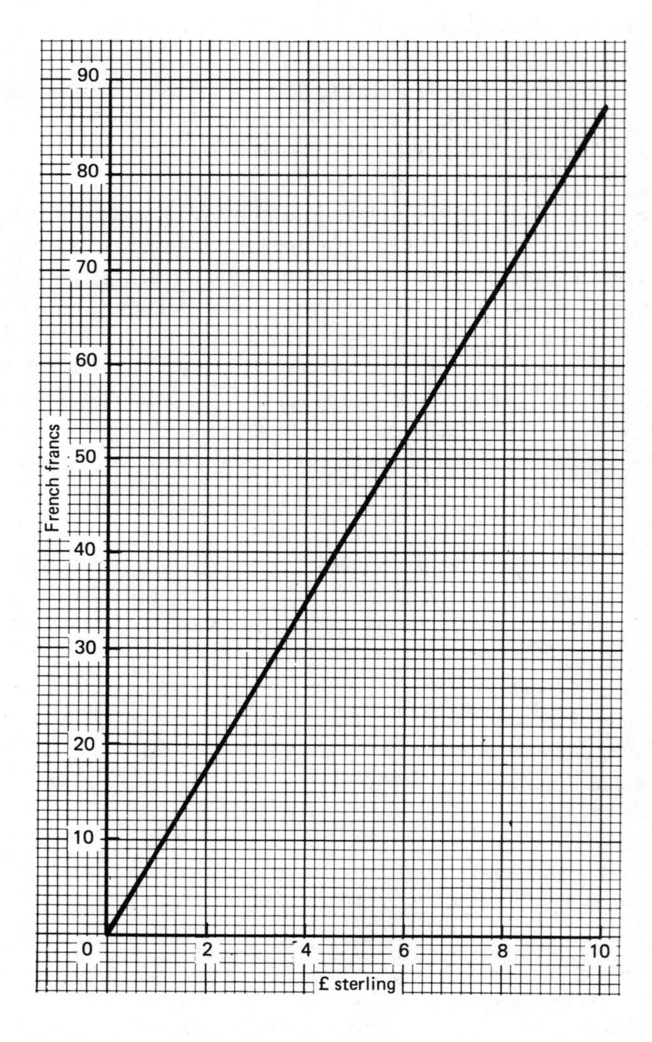

FIGURE 2.19 *Graph for converting francs/£ sterling – 8.75 francs to £*

More questions for the group

1 Do you think the graph is more useful than a pocket calculator for these sorts of transactions?

2 What are the limitations of the graph in this sort of calculation?

39 THE CONTINENTAL TOUR

Judi Pirelli is a folk-singer and last summer she decided to have a working holiday on the Continent. Her agent arranged a number of engagements for her and she kept a log of her financial transactions during the tour. The basic details are set out below and you are invited to discover how much she brought back home at the end of the tour:

17 June	Arrived in Rotterdam with £200 which was exchanged for guilders at a rate of 4.32 to the £
21 ,,	Paid for 3 days in hotel at 28 guilders per day Spent 34.50 guilders on sundries
22 ,,	Received 100 guilders for 2 performances at the Englander Club, Rotterdam Left for Bonn – exchanged all currency into marks (100 guilders = 96.50 marks)
26 ,,	Paid for 4 days in hotel at 25 marks per day Spent 155.25 marks on sundries Received 300 marks for 6 performances at Mitzi Brun's in Bonn Exchanged all marks for £ (at 4.03 marks to the £)
27 ,,	Started tour of British Army camps
30 ,,	Spent £80.75 on clothes Charged £3.85 per day for 3 days' billets Received £25.50 for each of 6 performances Exchanged all sterling for French francs (at 9.42 francs to the £)
2 July	Spent 63 francs on cosmetics and perfumes
3 ,,	Paid for 4 days in Paris hotel at 85 francs per day Received 225 francs for each of 4 performances Exchanged all francs into £ (at 9.25 francs to the £) Spent £5.75 on the journey home

Some further calculations

1 If Judi put what was left of her money into a Building Society which paid interest at 6½% per annum and kept it there for six months, how much interest would she collect?

2 After Judi has been home for a few weeks she receives a letter from Mitzi Brun in Bonn offering her a three-month contract for a nightly show starting in the autumn. Mitzi Brun quotes a figure of 8500 marks. Judi is delighted and feverishly works out how much this would be worth to her. (Over the past few months the exchange rate has varied between 3.85 to 4.15 marks to the £.) What answer should she have arrived at?

Questions for the group to consider

1 Why do you think the Government sometimes limits the amount of money its people can spend abroad?

2 Why do you think the exchange rates vary according to whether you are buying or selling a currency?

3 How many foreign currencies can the group name?

40 COSTS AND RETURNS

Robert Saxby works for Dextra Chemical Ltd as a research chemist, but he has always hankered after a career in journalism. Now he has been given the chance to show his prowess. Dextra have given him permission to publish a monthly news sheet. The only proviso is that the project should be treated as a commercial venture. Robert has no objection to that. He has a methodical nature and he carefully lists the various items of expenditure and the expected receipts from the sales of the news sheets:

(i) the rent of the printing machine will amount to £60 per month, and the cost will be incurred even if no printing is done:

(ii) the cost of the paper will amount to £2.50 per 1000 sheets and each copy of the news sheet will contain 10 sheets, or 20 pages;

(iii) the cost of printing ink (in two colours) is estimated at £1.70 per 1000 sheets;

(iv) four local firms have agreed to insert small advertisements regularly. It is expected that they will pay a total of £10 for advertisements in each issue (£2.50 each); and

(v) the suggested price of each news sheet is 5p per copy.

Robert decides to draw up a table setting out the costs at various levels of production:

No. of copies produced	Cost of machine	Cost of paper	Cost of ink	Total cost
1000				
2000				
3000				
4000				
5000				
6000				
7000				

Complete this table for Robert – and then do the same to the next one. This sets out the receipts which Robert could expect at different levels of circulation:

No. of copies sold	Advertising revenue	Proceeds (5p per copy)	Total returns
1000			
2000			
3000			
4000			
5000			
6000			
7000			

Armed with this information Robert needs to find out how many news sheets he will have to sell in order to cover his costs (i.e. to break even). Plot the totals you have obtained for costs and returns on the graph in Figure 2.20. How many will Robert need to sell in order to cover the costs of production?

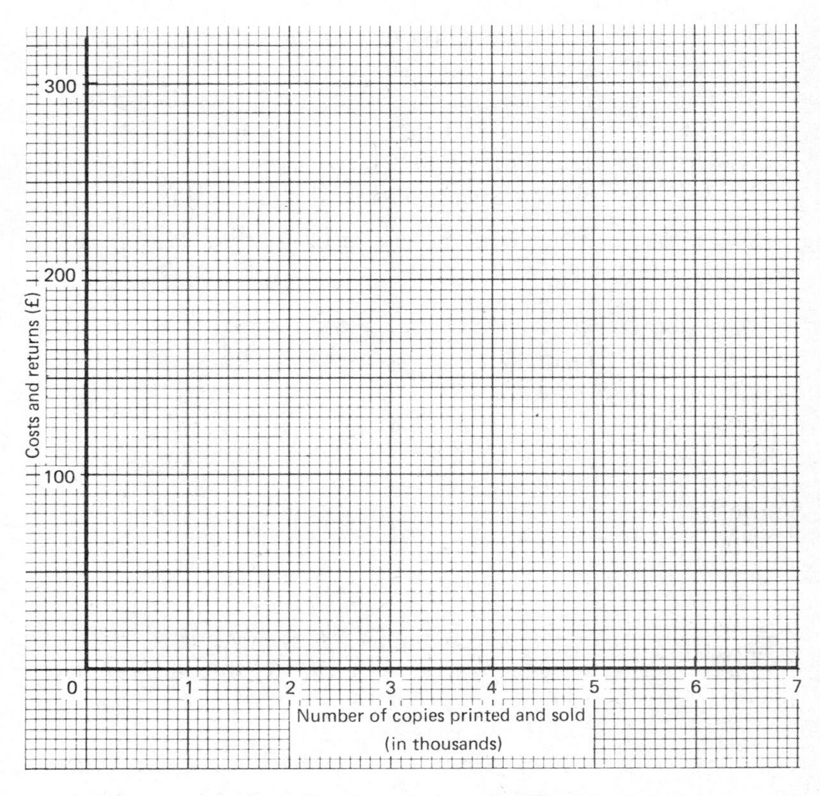

FIGURE 2.20 *Break-even chart for Dextra news sheet*

Questions for group discussion

1 Do you think the advertisers might be persuaded to pay more if the circulation increases? Why?
2 Do you think the employees of Dextra will mind paying for a news sheet? Do you think it would be better, generally, to have a glossier magazine-type production, charging a higher price, or a smaller and even cheaper publication?
3 Robert Saxby is allowed to work on the news sheet for three hours a week instead of doing his normal work. What do you think Dextra hope to get out of the news sheet?

3 Speed and Accuracy Tests

However much one theorises about statistics and mathematics, in the end one has to come to the point where calculations have to be performed. These are the mechanical operations, but speed and accuracy are essential. Of course one can use pocket calculators, but even sophisticated computers in this Age of Technology, but there are obvious dangers in becoming too dependent on such devices. What happens when we have left our calculator behind, or the batteries run down? What happens to our sophisticated computers when the power supplies are cut off? Are we to be left with a mental vacuum?

This section of the work represents an effort to develop the essential mechanical skills in basic calculations which is essential to success in business.

The aim here is to indicate some of the mechanical exercises which can be practised, but tutors may wish to produce further exercises on loose sheets where they feel their students would benefit from additional exercises of this nature.

PERCENTAGES, FRACTIONS AND DECIMALS

Complete the following table wherever figures are omitted:

Percentages	Fractions	Decimals (to 2 places)
100%	1	1.00
50%	½	
75%		0.75
	¼	0.25
	⅛	
		0.1

Percentages	Fractions	Decimals (to 2 places)
5%		
	1/16	
22½%		
		0.03
15%		
	1/40	
		0.15
	1/3	
45%		
	1/12	
		0.35
	2/25	
17½%		
	3/8	
		1.65
1 3/8%		
	7/8	
		0.01
	5/16	
2¾%		
	7/16	
		1.05
	9/16	
4 7/8%		
	11/16	
		10.11
	1/32	
98%		
	3/32	
		3.75

PICK THE WINNER

You are allowed a total of 5 minutes to indicate – in the fourth column – which figure in each row you think is the largest in the row. So, if you think 10% of £72 is larger than 5/8 of £64.80 or than 2.4 x £14.50, you will put a C in the fourth column.

Then you will work out the various calculations to see if your first estimates were right. A fifth column has been provided so that you can change your mind and put another letter down, if your calculations show you were wrong the first time. You may use calculators for this part of the exercise.

	A	B	C		
(1)	5/8 of £64.80	2.4 x £14.50	10% of £72	C	A
(2)	3/8 of £43.00	1.9 x £7.50	8% of £120		
(3)	¾ of £45.76	2.85 x £46	19% of £90		
(4)	5/8 of £120	3.9 x £66.30	27% of £88		
(5)	3/16 of £75	5.7 x £1.65	56% of £28		
(6)	5/16 of £63.25	3.75 x £6	39% of £50		
(7)	4/5 x £61.35	5.56 x £9.25	3% of £950		
(8)	7/8 x £3.15	0.9 x £3.25	2½ % of £98		
(9)	5/8 x £100.56	17.5 x £4.75	55% of £90		
(10)	3/8 x £1.05	1.05 x £0.375	11% of £12		
(11)	7/12 of £3.50	1.15 x £1.55	7½% of £50		
(12)	4/5 of £19.90	10.5 x £1.15	3½% of £45		
(13)	¾ of £56.56	1.05 x £41.15	4½% of £92		
(14)	¾ of £11.15	15.6 x £0.50	35% of £15		
(15)	1/8 of £45.45	1.85 x £4.15	25% of £19		
(16)	¼ of £34.56	1.7 x £10.35	9% of £8.70		
(17)	3/16 of £75	4.5 x £5.50	85% of £11.15		
(18)	5/8 of £0.63	0.05 x £7.75	3½% of £14.25		
(19)	7/8 of £1.05	0.03 x £25.50	7½% of £31		
(20)	5/8 of £99	6.5 x £9.75	56% of £100		
(21)	1/8 of $15	0.12 x $22	15% of $16.25		
(22)	7/8 of $0.78	1.15 x $0.65	5% of $35.35		
(23)	¼ of $175	7.65 x $5.56	38% of $95		
(24)	3/16 of $88	9.75 x $2.15	95% of $256		

TIME TRIAL

You are challenged to add all the columns and rows below within the time limit of 25 minutes. (Columns go down, rows go across.)

						(£)
£23.17 +	3.45 +	11.56 +	6.57 +	5.05	=	
3.44 +	106.34 +	103.56 +	34.34 +	18.78	=	
5.66 +	15.45 +	34.23 +	7.66 +	4.45	=	
11.25 +	8.96 +	7.96 +	9.45 +	11.04	=	
8.87 +	10.06 +	1.06 +	1.10 +	0.05	=	
Sub-totals						

6.66 +	3.34 +	7.15 +	1.15 +	1.34	=	
0.45 +	0.09 +	1.18 +	3.33 +	9.09	=	
2.20 +	3.20 +	2.34 +	77.75 +	88.85	=	
76.75 +	4.50 +	5.50 +	1.16 +	1.19	=	
7.17 +	6.75 +	3.34 +	9.99 +	1.11	=	
Sub-totals						

9.15 +	4.25 +	6.96 +	0.15 +	10.00	=	
5.15 +	10.00 +	1.10 +	0.19 +	5.55	=	
4.56 +	3.34 +	16.65 +	9.95 +	9.97	=	
8.85 +	8.86 +	25.25 +	8.86 +	8.15	=	
35.35 +	5.11 +	5.23 +	23.25 +	70.00	=	
Sub-totals						

4.44 +	3.17 +	4.56 +	44.42 +	3.43	=	
13.75 +	24.00 +	8.87 +	7.76 +	9.96	=	
6.54 +	8.76 +	8.43 +	6.45 +	8.88	=	
65.75 +	1.45 +	6.66 +	4.43 +	3.44	=	
66.24 +	4.32 +	3.34 +	3.56 +	11.11	=	
Sub-totals						

					£
25.35 +	25.00 +	44.45 +	45.55 +	6.63 =	
76.23 +	5.47 +	11.12 +	8.89 +	2.35 =	
46.12 +	5.56 +	7.77 +	6.67 +	5.66 =	
108.13 +	5.78 +	22.23 +	0.22 +	2.25 =	
111.50 +	6.34 +	2.22 +	6.23 +	1.19 =	
£	£	£	£	£	£

Totals

ADD AND CHECK

You are invited to pair up for this exercise. One of you will deal with Section A, arriving at the Grand Total as soon as possible. The other will deal with Section B. When you have both completed your sections you should pass your calculations to your partner for checking. Who has made the most mistakes? Who has found the most mistakes?

Section A (£)

£2.45 +	4.56 +	6.06 +	8.76 +	1.78 +	3.34 =	
£1.16 +	11.07 +	0.08 +	22.65 +	78.11 +	5.56 =	
£9.19 +	22.34 +	19.19 +	22.25 +	72.26 +	6.66 =	
£8.08 +	99.09 +	1.01 +	16.17 +	25.05 +	25.76 =	
£6.45 +	1.99 +	1.64 +	4.46 +	4.64 +	0.46 =	
£7.67 +	81.19 +	0.18 +	0.19 +	1.19 +	9.19 =	
					Sub-total	£
£9.09 +	1.17 +	2.54 +	33.67 +	33.56 +	3.89 =	
£6.78 +	0.98 +	1.78 +	43.67 +	83.89 +	1.89 =	
£0.07 +	5.59 +	75.67 +	78.88 +	1.88 +	1.88 =	
£4.78 +	1.11 +	6.89 +	1.15 +	5.12 +	1.18 =	
£2.34 +	6.89 +	35.34 +	5.11 +	65.13 +	91.87 =	
£6.66 +	19.20 +	66.66 +	102.15 +	111.50 +	0.01 =	
					Grand Total =	£

Section B

							(£)
£4.05 +	6.75 +	8.76 +	4.50 +	3.45 +	1.50	=	
£1.60 +	12.34 +	73.65 +	12.35 +	55.45 +	16.87	=	
£4.65 +	77.76 +	5.69 +	19.91	+109.01 +	6.08	=	
£6.75 +	66.00 +	1.19 +	1.09 +	88.19 +	1.29	=	
£1.86 +	2.69 +	3.56 +	100.05 +	64.46 +	8.18	=	
£1.78 +	1.89 +	35.25 +	88.09	+100.01 +	5.55	=	
					Sub-total	=	£
£9.00 +	3.69 +	8.15 +	5.16 +	17.70 +	70.70	=	
£1.00 +	1.50 +	1.86 +	171.85 +	65.09 +	11.11	=	
£6.66 +	55.00 +	21.20 +	75.02 +	2.12	+100.00	=	
£8.50 +	60.00 +	33.34 +	100.05 +	76.50 +	45.00	=	
£1.75 +	35.19 +	7.60 +	11.45 +	11.35	+205.05	=	
£5.55 +	75.75 +	3.57 +	225.25	+100.00 +	22.55	=	
					Grand Total	=	£

CALL, COPY AND ADD

Form pairs. The first person should read out (as quietly as possible) List A below. The second person should copy down the figures without seeing the list. When this has been done the second person should read out List B to the first person. They should then each add their own list. Then the two should switch lists and check both the calculations *and* the figures (to make sure they have been copied down correctly).

List A

1	2	3	4
(£)	(£)	(£)	(£)
1000.56	40.36	18.20	7.77
202.02	901.09	224.42	13.30
343.67	45.54	8.07	4.04
11.09	56.88	55.05	40.14
118.17	56.88	6.98	111.11
£	£	£	£

5	6	7	8
(£)	(£)	(£)	(£)
71.00	87.87	19.19	2560.05
111.05	234.34	99.99	45.43
67.52	0.25	0.36	0.34
775.00	10.16	4.40	6.16
84.56	22.02	5.55	19.90
£	£	£	£

List B

1	2	3	4
(£)	(£)	(£)	(£)
3.45	40.14	47.34	18.88
19.50	0.67	1.40	0.67
6.66	345.80	5.65	18.80
17.78	768.19	167.04	0.90
119.35	0.05	440.14	0.01
£	£	£	£

5	6	7	8
(£)	(£)	(£)	(£)
1000.00	17.77	66.06	2010.10
100.19	8.18	222.02	887.78
200.04	100.10	44.40	13.31
14.40	33.34	43.43	0.18
0.04	7.17	0.50	4.04
£	£	£	£

If further practice is required, the previous exercise can also be used in this fashion.

MULTIPLY AND SUBTRACT

Multiply the figure in Column A by the figure in Column B. Put the result in Column C. Subtract the figure in Column D from the figure in Column C. Put the result in Column E. Complete the sub-totals and then the Grand Total.

A (£)	B	C (£)	D (£)	E (£)
12.30	3		4.45	
11.12	5		6.75	
2.35	7		7.75	
46.80	3		45.00	
0.34	16		1.08	
5.87	7		2.89	
			Sub-total	
22.02	2.5		0.99	
10.00	3.5		5.65	
2.25	5		11.15	
1.18	9		8.88	
5.66	11		50.00	
76.05	2.4		87.87	
			Sub-total	
0.66	10		5.56	
3.35	6		9.98	
98.09	3		198.75	
2.34	5		9.06	
11.00	2.25		19.95	
6.79	9		53.35	
			Sub-total	
24.12	3.5		11.01	
25.50	2.7		6.75	
60.75	7.7		305.50	
88.00	2.15		99.90	
72.62	2.7		0.99	
1.81	0.5		0.09	
			Sub-total	

A (£)	B	C (£)	D (£)	E (£)
			Sub-total	
65.56	1.2		0.99	
15.51	4.2		2.20	
14.50	2.4		2.02	
41.50	3.5		0.22	
15.50	6.15		1.16	
105.00	2.5		3.30	
			Grand Total	£

DIVIDE AND ADD

Divide the figure in Column A by the figure in Column B. Put the result in Column C and add this to the figure in Column D. Put the final result in Column E. Complete the sub-totals and the Grand Total.

A (£)	B	C (£)	D (£)	E (£)
770.00	2.5		100.00	
65.00	7.2		11.50	
110.75	3.9		9.75	
99.00	2.5		18.80	
112.25	3.5		1.18	
75.75	2.7		3.35	
			Sub-total	
500.00	1.5		7.05	
19.20	2.4		8.10	
24.50	2.7		6.85	
35.00	3.5		3.76	
105.00	2.5		5.01	
95.00	1.5		10.10	
			Sub-total	
24.00	3.5		1.01	
25.50	2.7		6.75	
60.75	7.7		5.05	
88.00	2.5		1.11	
72.60	2.7		0.99	
1.80	0.5		2.50	
			Sub-total	

A (£)	B	C (£)	D (£)	D (£)
			Sub-total	
16.00	2.7		1.10	
94.88	3.5		3.15	
10.00	2.5		2.25	
13.35	1.75		5.75	
24.65	2.5		1.05	
105.05	3.75		6.60	
			Sub-total	
600.00	1.5		5.00	
15.00	3.5		1.60	
75.65	2.7		12.51	
5.05	2.5		100.00	
11.55	3.5		1.10	
1.55	2.5		0.25	
			Grand Total	£

METER READINGS

Study the table below. The first three items have been calculated for you. Complete the rest of the table along the same lines.

Previous meter reading	Present meter reading	Units consumed	Price per unit (p)	Charge (£)
37214	38317	1103	2.0	22.06
5346	5472	126	2.6	3.28
116578	117098	520	3.1	16.12
14436	17008		2.0	
5784	7032		2.0	
11136	12978		2.6	
9979	11078		3.1	
235840	246979		2.6	
			Total A	£

Previous meter reading	Present meter reading	Units consumed	Price per unit (p)	Charge (£)
66752	67511		2.0	
69356	69871		2.6	
75831	80002		2.6	
98399	110041		3.1	
56347	60856		2.6	
584	2385		3.1	
98799	107223		2.6	
1567	2911		3.1	
			Total B	£
9986	11004		3.1	
6549	7939		2.6	
7989	8037		3.1	
8946	10072		2.0	
8657	11053		2.6	
7481	8910		2.0	
990	1981		2.5	
9191	11089		3.1	
			Total C	£
1700	1899		2.0	
23774	29191		3.1	
9761	11080		2.6	
10044	19404		3.1	
7557	9444		2.6	
133098	140382		3.1	
8802	10193		2.6	
36616	39119		3.1	
			Total D	£

FOREIGN EXCHANGE HANDICAP I

Split into pairs for another contest. This time one of each pair of contestants will use a calculator to convert various currencies into £ sterling. His opponent will work out the conversions unaided, but to equalise the burden this contestant will only need to complete Section A. The contestant using the calculator will have to complete both sections.

The rates of exchange are: (i) 26.70 Austrian schillings to £; (ii) 8.40 French francs to £; (iii) 4.10 West German marks to £; (iv) 1.55 South African rands to £.

Convert the following currencies into £ sterling

Section A		(£)	Section B		(£)
65 francs	=		195 marks	=	
95 marks	=		14 francs	=	
13 rands	=		78 schillings	=	
98 marks	=		107 francs	=	
186 francs	=		765 marks	=	
77 francs	=		32 schillings	=	
225 rands	=		156 rands	=	
76 marks	=		58 schillings	=	
111 schillings	=		66 francs	=	
32 marks	=		47 marks	=	
279 schillings	=		9 marks	=	
109 marks	=	______	198 francs	=	______
Sub-total	=		*Sub-total*	=	
49 francs	=		57 francs	=	
333 marks	=		98 schillings	=	
225 schillings	=		17 rands	=	
77 rands	=		44 rands	=	
550 rands	=		9 marks	=	
112 marks	=		775 francs	=	
12 francs	=		45 schillings	=	
225 schillings	=		95 rands	=	
13 marks	=		9 marks	=	

Section A		(£)	Section B		(£)
75 francs	=		80 francs	=	
100 marks	=		50 rands	=	
55 francs	=	______	63 francs	=	______
Total	=	======	*Total*	=	======

(Note that each calculation is required to be made separately.)

FOREIGN EXCHANGE HANDICAP II

The rules for this exercise are the same as in the previous one except that both contestants will be able to check their calculations as they go by referring to the accompanying graphs (Figures 3.1 and 3.2).

The rates of exchange are: (i) 143.75 Spanish pesetas to £; (ii) 74.50 Portuguese escudos to £.

Convert the following sums into £ sterling

Section A		(£)	Section B		(£)
400 escudos	=		700 pesetas	=	
100 escudos	=		100 pesetas	=	
335 pesetas	=		275 escudos	=	
75 escudos	=		65 pesetas	=	
270 pesetas	=		110 pesetas	=	
90 escudos	=		55 escudos	=	
325 escudos	=		175 pesetas	=	
650 pesetas	=		320 escudos	=	
175 escudos	=		140 escudos	=	
200 escudos	=		355 pesetas	=	
155 escudos	=		250 escudos	=	
200 pesetas	=	______	70 pesetas	=	______
Total	=	======	*Total*	=	======

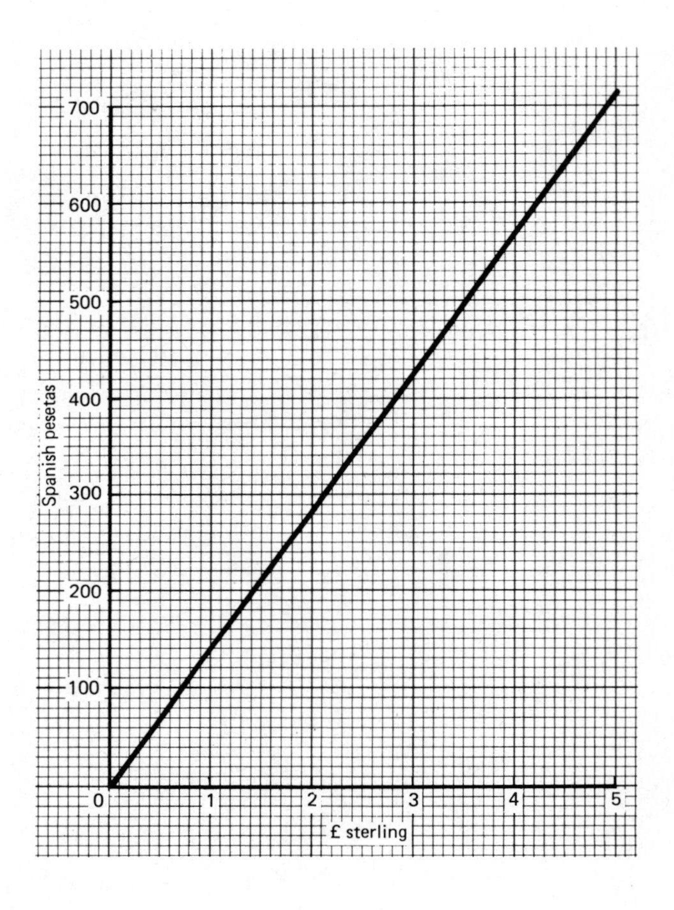

FIGURE 3.1 *Graph for converting pesetas/£ sterling – 143.75 pesetas to £*

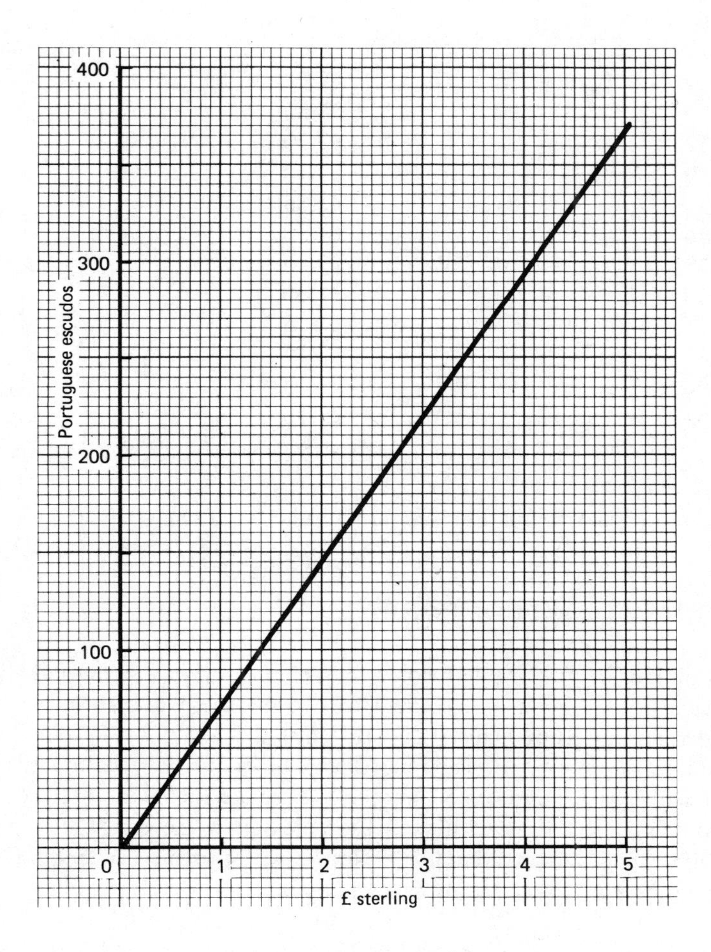

FIGURE 3.2 *Graph for converting escudos/£ sterling – 74.50 escudos to £*

Convert £ sterling into pesetas/escudos at the rates given

Section A		(pesetas)	Section B		(escudos)
£3.25	=		£5	=	
£4.60	=		£2.50	=	
£3.50	=		£2.10	=	
£2.10	=		£3.40	=	
£4.30	=		£2.65	=	
£4.75	=		£1.80	=	
£3.10	=		£3.50	=	
£1.10	=		£1.60	=	
£3.75	=		£3.75	=	
£1.65	=		£2.25	=	
£4.90	=		£3.25	=	
£3.65	=	______	£1.40	=	______
Total	=	======	*Total*	=	======

(Note that each calculation is required to be made separately.)

CONVERT AND COMPARE

In column A of the table below you will find various units of foreign currency. First, you are required to convert these foreign currencies into £ sterling using Figures 2.19 (p. 120), 3.1 and 3.2 only. Put your estimates in column B. Then perform your calculations arithmetically and see how accurately you were able to make the coversions, i.e. by comparing the results with your estimates from the graphs. Put your arithmetic results in column C. Note any differences in column D. Finally, you are asked to add up and derive a total for column C.

The rates of exchange are: (i) 143.75 pesetas to £; (ii) 8.75 francs to £; (iii) 74.50 escudos to £.

	A	B	C	D
Escudos	60.00			
	85.00			
	105.00			
	250.00			
	450.00			

	A	B	C	D
	19.50			
	57.20			
	66.66			
Pesetas	150.00			
	76.00			
	105.00			
	15.00			
	300.00			
	75.50			
	450.75			
	135.75			
Francs	65.00			
	85.00			
	115.00			
	19.00			
	100.00			
	17.50			
	224.70			
	55.55			

AVERAGES

Study each of the following 9 columns. Decide which of them contains the higher figures on average. Tick the box of your choice at the foot of the columns. Then work out the averages (*arithmetic means*) for each column and see whether you chose correctly. Then underline the *median* figure in each column, and the *mode* over the whole series.

A	B	C
16.5	22.76	17.25
8.8	18.5	2.5
118.55	45.5	33.6
7.75	11.7	9.9
25.0	16.5	16.5
16.5	33.4	8.8
105.6	42.4	7.75

D	E	F
78.3	33.4	2.5
66.6	25.0	25.0
80.25	11.7	9.9
8.8	8.8	16.5
16.5	11.7	9.9
8.8	16.5	45.5
25.0	8.9	8.8
45.5	33.4	2.5
22.76	11.7	66.6

G	H	I
22.76	17.25	105.6
2.5	33.4	2.5
7.75	18.5	16.5
8.08	8.1	9.9
105.6	80.4	33.6
16.5	33.6	16.5
7.75	16.5	7.75
8.8	17.25	33.5
22.6	8.8	33.4
16.5	33.6	8.6
8.6	16.5	8.8

A	B	C	D	E	F	G	H	I
☐	☐	☐	☐	☐	☐	☐	☐	☐

THE GLADIATORS I

This exercise is designed for the use of pocket calculators. The group should be split into two. One half will be able to use pocket calculators. These will be called ‘The Lions’. The other half will be ‘The Gladiators’ and will pit their unaided skills against their mechanised opponents. Gladiators and Lions will be paired off by the tutor and the contest will be between each pair of students. Each Gladiator and his opponent will work through the following calculations as quickly and accurately as they can. Whichever of them, Lion or Gladiator, finishes the exercise first wins the contest. Of course, if the wrong answer is produced to the tutor, the contest is awarded to the opponent.

When all the contests have been completed it will be interesting to see how many of the Gladiators have survived.

The contest (work to the nearest penny)

		(£)			(£)
1½% of £105	=		6½% of £88	=	
1⅝% of £120	=		6¾% of £1100	=	
11½% of £56	=		7½% of £50.50	=	
10% of £1005	=		5½% of £3.75	=	
4½% of £40	=		2½% of £90	=	
6% of £60.15	=		12% of £13	=	
Sub-total	(i)		*Sub-total*	(ii)	
1⅞% of £14.15	=		15% of £40	=	
5% of £50.50	=		12½% of £35	=	
6% of £10	=		7% of £13	=	
8% of £19	=		6⅝% of £45	=	
7½% of £25	=		5% of £30	=	
8% of £1150	=		6% of £155	=	
Sub-total	(iii)		*Sub-total*	(iv)	
15% of £15	=				
7⅛% of £10	=		Sub-total (i)	=	
12½% of £19	=		,, ,, (ii)	=	
1½% of £450	=		,, ,, (iii)	=	
1¾% of £2.25	=		,, ,, (iv)	=	
4½% of £1.75	=		,, ,, (v)	=	
Sub-total	(v)		*Grand Total*	=	

THE GLADIATORS II

This is another contest between Lions and Gladiators. Both contestants are asked to bear in mind the following:

(i) when you see a small number above and to the right of a figure – thus 3^2 – this is 3 squared, or $3 \times 3 = 9$, while $4^3 = 4 \times 4 \times 4 = 64$; and

(ii) when you find figures enclosed in a bracket – thus $(\frac{1}{2} \times 1.1)^2$ – this sum has to be worked out before further calculations are made. So, $\pounds 1.5 + (\frac{1}{2} \times \pounds 1.2)^2/4 = \pounds 1.59$.

The contest (work to the nearest penny)

		(£)			(£)
$\pounds 2.50 \times \frac{7}{16}$	=		$\pounds 3.45 \times \frac{3}{5}$	=	
$4.5 \times \pounds 5.65$	=		$6\frac{1}{2}\%$ of £1050	=	
$\pounds 1.75^2$	=		$\pounds 4 + (\frac{3}{8} \times \pounds 2.4)^2/3$	=	
£3.45 – £1.46	=		$\pounds 7.86 \times 4$	=	
$7\frac{1}{2}\%$ of £106	=		$5\frac{1}{2}\%$ of £32.75	=	
$\frac{\pounds 10.15}{3.5}$	=		$\frac{\pounds 25.25}{2.5}$	=	
$\frac{7}{8} \times \pounds 3.75$	=		$8\frac{1}{2}\%$ of £55	=	
$\pounds 1.1^3$	=		$\pounds 3.50\,(1.1 + 0.8)^2/5$	=	
$5\frac{1}{2}\%$ of £60	=		$7\frac{1}{2}\%$ of £45.75	=	
$\pounds 18.35 - \pounds 2\frac{1}{8}$	=		8% of £100.65	=	
Sub-total	(i)		*Sub-total*	(ii)	

$\pounds 6.60 \times \frac{1}{25}$	=				
15% of £50	=				
$\pounds 2.65^2$	=				
$\frac{\pounds 45.25}{1.5}$	=				
$\frac{\pounds 4.75 \times (1.3)^2}{5}$	=				
1% of £5	=		Sub-total (i)	=	
$12\frac{1}{2}\%$ of £2.15	=		" " (ii)	=	
$\pounds 4.15 \times 2.3$	=		" " (iii)	=	
$\frac{\pounds 5.55 \times 2.7}{3}$	=				
$8\frac{1}{2}\%$ of £302	=				
Sub-total	(iii)		*Grand Total*		

DEBITS AND CREDITS I

This is a copy of a customer's bank statement, i.e. a copy of his account in the books of the bank.

Whenever there is a figure in the debit column below you take that figure from the previous balance. When there is a figure in the credit column you add that figure to the previous balance. The first few calculations have been made for you, and you are now invited to complete the remaining balances.

	Debit (£)	Credit (£)	Balance (£)
2 Jan			37.56
3	7.65		29.91
4		57.34	87.25
5	24.55		
6		3.46	
9		105.05	
10	4.75	2.43	
11	16.78		
12		55.00	
13		73.42	
16	1.99		
17	2.98		
18		6.76	
19		98.54	
20	2.65	1.50	
23	18.88		
24	7.45		
25	30.10		
26		7.55	
		3.75	
30		1.16	
31	1.75		
1 Feb	2.25	5.50	
2	6.75		
3		20.20	
6		5.15	
7	8.76		
8		3.65	
9	5.75		
10		10.15	

As a check on your work, total the debit and credit columns. Add the total of the credits to the starting balance. Take the total debits from the new total. This should give you the same figure as your final balance, i.e. that for 10 February.

DEBITS AND CREDITS II

Use the same techniques as in the previous exercise. At one point the balance will be a debit one. This is what happens when your account becomes overdrawn at the bank. Think carefully when you come to work out the balances at that stage.

	Debit (£)	Credit (£)	Balance (£)
5 June			1186.75
6	68.76		
7	181.64	1.75	
9	26.86		
10	117.91	5.55	
14	352.56		
15	10.00		
16	10.00		
17	10.00		
18	388.99		
19	65.05	1.12	
20	357.75		
22	4.15	7.77	
23		15.00	
24	10.00	5.00	
	1.75		
27	227.65		
28		98.50	
30		365.00	
2 July	5.65	35.25	
3	64.65	1.65	
4	4.75	98.00	
5	3.34	101.15	
7		54.10	
8	5.05		

9 July		75.00
10	11.12	88.85
12	6.56	375.00
13	1.75	219.25
14	3.30	1078.78
15	125.75	
16	19.19	100.00
17	8.50	

Check your final balances (for 17 July) as you did in the previous example.

THE SATELLITE

A particular component used in a new communication satellite can take the form of four different shapes and materials according to designs produced in various countries. They are all equally effective so the choice is to be determined by cost. The shapes of the alternative units are shown in Figure 3.3 (a–d) and are accompanied by their descriptions, their countries of origin and their cost per square centimetre. Which would be the cheapest to use on this evidence? The rates of exchange to be used are: (i) $1.95 to £, (ii) 8.50 francs to £; (ii) 4.15 marks to £.

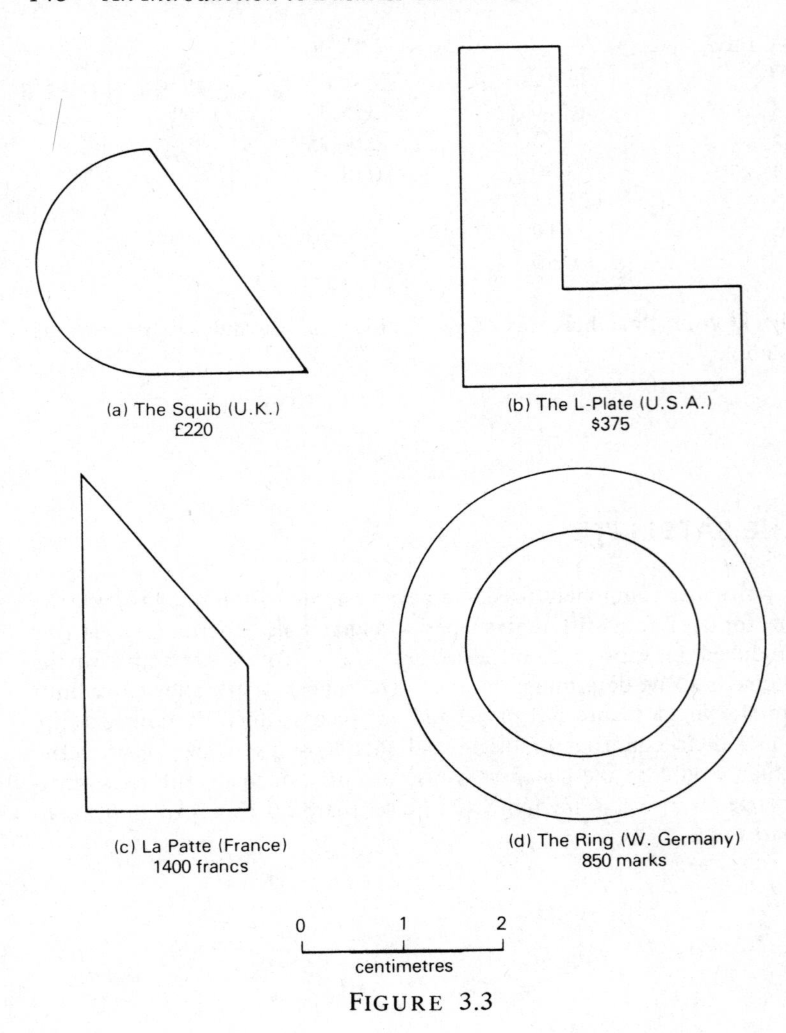
(a) The Squib (U.K.)
£220
(b) The L-Plate (U.S.A.)
$375
(c) La Patte (France)
1400 francs
(d) The Ring (W. Germany)
850 marks
0
1
2
centimetres

FIGURE 3.3

4 Conventional Examination Work

First, an acknowledgement. Gratitude is expressed both to the Royal Society of Arts and the London Chamber of Commerce and Industry Ltd, whose examining boards have kindly allowed various questions from their past examination papers to be included here.

I also express my gratitude to the Business Education Council for allowing me to include their Specimen Examination paper in Business Calculations for their General Award. This is reproduced in full on the final pages.

As part of their training programme the majority of business students are required to take conventional examinations in order to prove their level of attainment, both to employers and themselves. The assignments which have been undertaken in Section 2 and the mechanical exercises in Section 3 should have equipped students who have proceeded this far to take conventional examinations in their stride.

There are four particular examinations which have been catered for here, in addition to those of the Business Education Council:

1 The Royal Society of Arts – Arithmetic – Stage 1 (Elementary)
2 ,, ,, ,, ,, ,, ,, – Stage 2 (Intermediate)
3 ,, ,, ,, ,, ,, – Business Calculations (Certificate in Office Studies)
4 The London Chamber of Commerce and Industry – Arithmetic (Elementary Stage).

The source of the questions that follow is indicated in the brackets at the end of each, respectively

(1) R.S.A. 1 (2) R.S.A. 2 (3) R.S.A., C.O.S. (4) L.C.C. & I. Elem.

In each case the particular examination from which the question was extracted is also mentioned.

This section is divided into two parts. In the first each question is followed by a fully worked solution, while in the second the questions

are posed but it is left to the students to arrive at the answers unaided.
One way to tackle the first part would be to:

(i) copy out the question to be dealt with, then
(ii) close the book and work out your own solution, and
(iii) when you have arrived at your solution turn back to the book and compare the workings.

Once more, may I emphasise the importance of neatness and clarity in setting out your answers, with adequate, but not excessive, 'labelling' of each step.

QUESTIONS WITH WORKINGS

1 An ice-cream salesman receives commission of 25% of the value of the ice-cream he sells. Find:
(a) the commission he receives when he sells ice-cream worth £30.40;
(b) the value of the ice-cream he has sold when his commission is £17.90.

(L.C.C. & I. Elem., Winter 1978)

Solution

(a) $25\% = \frac{1}{4}$ $\quad \frac{1}{4}$ of $\pounds 30.40 = \frac{\pounds 30.40}{4} = \pounds 7.60$

(b) If 25% of sales = £17.90

then 1% ,, ,, $= \frac{\pounds 17.90}{25}$

and 100% ,, ,, $= \frac{\pounds 17.90}{25} \times 100$

$= \frac{\pounds 17.90}{\not{2}\not{5}_{1}} \times \not{1}\not{0}\not{0}\ 4$

$= \pounds 71.60$

Or If $\frac{1}{4}$ of sales $= \pounds 17.90$
then $\frac{4}{4}$,, $= \pounds 17.90 \times 4$
$= \pounds 71.60$

2 The cost of production of certain articles was made up as follows: wages £650; materials £200; and other expenses £150. If wages increase by 10%, materials by 5% and other expenses by 4%, what will be the over-all percentage increase in the cost of production?

(R.S.A. 1, March 1978)

Solution

10% of £650 =	£65	Wages	£650
5% of £200 =	£10	Materials	£200
4% of £150 =	£6	Other expenses	£150
Total increase	£81	Original cost	£1000

$$\%\text{age increase} = \frac{81}{1000} \times 100 = \frac{81}{10} = 8.1\%$$

3 A man noticed that over a period of 13 weeks in three of the weeks his average weekly expenditure was £42, in four of the weeks his average weekly expenditure was £44, and in the remaining six weeks his average weekly expenditure was £45. Find:

(a) his total expenditure in those thirteen weeks; and
(b) his average weekly expenditure during the thirteen weeks.

(L.C.C. & I. Elem., Winter 1978)

Solution

(a)
3 weeks at £42 = 3 × 42 = £126
4 weeks at £44 = 4 × 44 = £176
6 weeks at £45 = 6 × 45 = £270
Total expenditure = £572

(b) Average expenditure = £572 ÷ 13

```
     44
13 ) 572
     52
      52
      52
      ..
```

i.e. average expenditure = £44 weekly

4 The sales in a department store for the first five months of a year were as follows: £3246, £2835, £2994, £3145 and £3416. What must be the value of the June sales in order to achieve a monthly average of £3250?

(R.S.A., C.O.S., June 1977)

Solution

If the average monthly sales are £3250
6 months' sales must total £3250 x 6 = £19500
The sales in the first five months total

£3246
2835
2994
3145
3416
£15636

The shortfall is £19500 – £15636 = £3864.
So the last months sales must be this amount to bring the total to £19500.

Answer = £3864

5 A man's salary is £2500 per annum. Before charging income tax the following allowances are deducted from his gross salary:

Personal allowance	£995
Child allowance	£515
Other allowances	£46

Calculate:
(a) his annual taxable income;
(b) his annual tax payable if the rate of tax is 35%;
(c) the percentage of his salary that is paid in tax.

(R.S.A., C.O.S., June 1976)

Solution

			(£)
(a)	Salary		=2500
	less Allowances	£995	
		515	
		46	1556
	Taxable income		= 944

(b) Tax of 35% on £944 $= \frac{35}{100} \times £944$
$= 3.5 \times £94.4$

94.4
3.5
283.2
47.2

£330.40 = *annual tax payable*

(c) *Percentage of salary in tax* =

$$\frac{330.4}{2500} \times 100 = 13.216\%$$

6 A bankrupt as assets of 7500 francs and liabilities of 12000 francs. Calculate the following:

(a) What fraction, in the lowest terms possible, can be paid to his creditors?

(b) What percentage of the amount owing does each creditor lose?

(c) How much does a creditor for 952 francs lose?

(d) A creditor receives 1485 francs. How much was the original debt?

(R.S.A. 2, June 1977)

Solution

(a) $\frac{7500}{1200} = \frac{75}{120} = \frac{15}{24} = \frac{5}{8}$

(b) Each creditor loses ⅜ of the amount owed to him, or 37½%

(c) 37½% of 952 francs is lost

25% of 952 = ¼ of 952, or $\frac{952}{4}$

= 238

12½% is ½ of 25% = $\frac{238}{2}$ = 119

357 francs

(d) If 1485 francs = 62½% of the amount owed

then $\frac{1485}{62.5}$ francs = 1% of that sum

and $\frac{1485}{62.5} \times 100$ francs = 100% of the amount

$\frac{1485}{62.5} \times 100 = \frac{14850}{6.25}$ = 2376 francs = *original amount owed.*

7 A businessman imported cloth from France for which he paid 8.95 francs a metre when the rate of exchange was £1 = 9.23 francs. At what price per metre, to the nearest penny, should he sell the cloth in Britain if he is to make a profit of 30% on his outlay?

(R.S.A., C.O.S., June 1976)

Solution

8.95 francs per metre was the outlay
a 30% increase on that would be 8.95 x 0.3
$8.95 \times 0.3 = 2.685$ francs
$8.95 + 2.685 = 11.635$ francs
11.635 frs would be the price required to produce a 30% profit
11.635 francs converted at 9.23 to the £

$$£\ \frac{11.635}{9.23} = £1.26 \text{ per metre}$$

8 In 1976 a young man enjoyed a touring holiday in West Germany. He spent money on:

(i) Petrol for 960 km; petrol costs 1.05 Deutschmarks per litre on an average of 10 km per litre.
(ii) Seven nights bed and breakfast at an average of 21 Deutschmarks per night.
(iii) Other meals and expenses averaged 26 Deutschmarks per day for eight days.
(iv) Presents and entertainment totalled 183 Deutschmarks.

If £1 = 3.90 Deutschmarks, what did his holiday cost in £ sterling?

(R.S.A. 2, March 1978)

Solution

(i) 10 km takes 1 litre of petrol
So 960 km would take 96 litres
96 litres at 1.05 DMs per litre
$= 1.05 \times 96 = 100.80$ DMs = cost of petrol

(ii) Bed and breakfast costs 7×21 DMs = 147 DMs.

(iii) Other meals and expenses 8×26 DMs = 208 DMs

(iv) *Total expenditure on holiday?*

Petrol	100.80
Bed and breakfast	147.00
Other meals and expenses	208.00
Presents, etc.	183.00
Total	638.80 DMs

At 3.90 DMs to the £, 638.80 DMs = $£\left(\frac{638.80}{3.90}\right)$

i.e. total cost of holiday = £163.80

9 The following table shows the number of cars coming off the assembly-line in a factory during each of 13 days:

Day	1	2	3	4	5	6	7	8	9	10	11	12	13
Number of cars	47	68	61	53	59	47	29	77	59	31	58	47	72

Find:
(a) the median;
(b) the mode;
(c) the arithmetical average number coming off daily, giving the answer to the nearest whole number; and
(d) the total profit on all the cars which came off the assembly-line during the 13 days, given that the profit on each is £120.

(R.S.A. 2, June 1977)

Solution

(a) There are 13 numbers in the series so in order to find the middle number arrange the figures in descending (or ascending) order. The *median* (or middle number) is 58.

77 72 68 61 59 59 $\underline{58}$ 53 47 47 47 31 29

(b) The most frequent output of cars in a day is 47 (this occurs 3 times in the series)

The *mode* is therefore 47

(c) To find the arithmetic average (*arithmetic mean*) add all the numbers in the series (47 + 68 + 61 + . . .)

708 cars are produced in 13 days
so average output per day is $\frac{708}{13}$
Average daily output = 54

(d) Profit = 708 cars (the total output) × £120 per car
708 × £120 = £84960
Profit = £84960

10 In a Borough the product of a penny rate is £235000. If the rate levied in one year is 65p in the £, calculate the total amount raised in rate income. If the total cost of running one of the

Borough's services is £910000, calculate, in pence correct to one place of decimals, how much of the 65p this represents.

(R.S.A., C.O.S., June 1977)

Solution

If 1 p rate produces £235000
a 65p ,, ,, £235000 x 65
= £15275000

If £15275000 is raised by a 65p rate

£1 ,, ,, ,, ,, $\frac{65}{15275000}$ p rate

£910000 ,, ,, ,, ,, $\frac{65 \times 910000}{15275000}$ p rate

= 3.9p (to one decimal place)

11 *A* and *B* enter into partnership, with *A* contributing £25000 as capital and *B* £5000. If B receives a salary as manager of the business of £4500 and the remaining profits are shared in proportion to the capital invested, how much will each partner receive in a year in which profits amount to £6840?

(R.S.A., C.O.S., June 1977)

Solution

Profits after salary is paid = £6840 less £4500 = £2340.

A receives $\frac{25000 \text{ (his capital)}}{30000 \text{ (total capital)}}$ x £2340 (remaining profit)

$= \frac{5}{6} \times £2340 = \frac{£11700}{6} = £1950$

B receives $\frac{1}{6} \times £2340 = £\ 390$

add salary = £4500

£4890

A receives £1950
B receives £4890

12 A new machine in a factory costs £2850. It is decided to depreciate its value each year by 15% of its book value at the beginning of the year. Calculate the book value after four complete years (give your answer to the nearest £10).

(R.S.A., C.O.S., June 1975)

Solution

Starting value = £2850
less depreciation in Year 1
10% of £2850 = £285
so 5% ,, ,, = £142.50 £427.50

Starting value in Year 2 = £2422.50
less depreciation in Year 2
10% of £2422.50 = £242.25
so 5% ,, ,, = £121.13 £363.38

Starting value in Year 3 = £2059.12
less depreciation in Year 3
10% of £2059.12 = £205.91
so 5% ,, ,, = £102.96 £308.87

Starting value in Year 4 = £1750.25
less depreciation in Year 4
10% of £1750.25 = £175.03
5% ,, ,, = £87.52 £262.55

Book value after 4 years = £1487.70
to nearest £10 = £1490

13 Calculate how much an investment of £2500 will amount to after 3 years if invested at 9% per annum compound interest, the interest being added annually (give your answer to the nearest £10).

(R.S.A., C.O.S., June 1977)

Solution

Principal at start = £2500
Interest for 1st year
$25\not{0}\not{0} \times \frac{9}{1\not{0}\not{0}}$ = £225

Principal at end of Year 1 = £2725
Interest for 2nd year
27.25 × 9 = £245.25

Principal at end of Year 2 = £2970.25

Interest for 3rd year

29.7025 x 9	= £267.32
Principal at end of Year 3	= £3237.57
to nearest £10	= £3240

14 A man owns £500 of a 5% Stock. He decides to sell this Stock when it is priced at £76 per £100 Stock and invests the proceeds in a bank deposit account which pays 7½% per annum interest. What will be the change in his annual income resulting from this transaction?

(R.S.A., C.O.S., June 1977)

Solution

The man's present income is 5% of £500 = £25 p.a.
He sells £500 Stock for £76 per £100 Stock
and receives 5 x £76 = £380 cash
Invested at 7½% per annum in bank deposit account

interest is 5% of £380 = 1/20th of £380	= £19
2½% ,, ,, = ½ x £19	= 9.50
New income p.a.	= £28.50

Increase in income = £3.50 p.a.

15 A dealer blends tea costing him 36p per lb with tea costing 46p per lb in the proportion of 6lb of the cheaper tea to 4lb of the dearer. At what price per pound must he sell the mixture in order to make a profit of 25% on his outlay?

(R.S.A., C.O.S., June 1975)

Solution

6 lb of tea at 36p per lb cost	£2.16
4 lb of tea at 46p per lb cost	£1.84
10 lb of mixed tea therefore cost	£4.00

which is 40p per lb

To make a profit of 25% he must sell the tea at ¼ over the cost,
i.e. 40p + 10p = 50p per lb

16 A room measures 6.5 metres long, 4.8 metres wide and 2.5 metres high. The four walls and ceiling are to be painted with *two* coats of emulsion paint which has a covering capacity of 15m^2 per litre. The paint costs £1.25 per litre and a one-litre tin is the smallest quantity supplied. (Allow 10m^2 for doors and windows.) Calculate:

(a) the area of the four walls and ceiling;
(b) the total area to be painted;
(c) the amount of the paint required to be purchased; and
(d) the cost of the paint.

(R.S.A., C.O.S., June 1976)

Solution

(a) Walls 1 and 2 = $(6.5 \times 2.5)\,2 = 32.5\text{m}^2$

Walls 3 and 4 = $(4.8 \times 2.5)\,2 = 24.0\text{m}^2$

56.5m^2

Ceiling = $6.5 \times 4.8 \quad = 31.2\text{m}^2$

87.7m^2

Area of walls and ceiling = 87.7m^2

(b) Area of walls and ceiling = 87.7m^2

less doors and windows = 10m^2

77.7m^2

There is an area of 77.7m^2 to be given two coats of paint, so area to be covered is

$77.7 \times 2 = 155.4\text{m}^2$

(c) 155.4m^2 to cover at 15m^2 per litre

$= \dfrac{155.4}{15}$ litre tins = 10.36 tins = 11 tins

(d) 11 litre tins cost £1.25 each

$11 \times £1.25 = £13.75$

QUESTIONS TO BE WORKED

1 (a) A bookseller buys a book for £3.00 and sells it to make a profit of 20% of his outlay. For how much did he sell the book?

(b) He sold for £4.50 another book that he had bought for £4.00. Find the profit he made as a percentage of his outlay.

(L.C.C. & I. Elem., Winter 1978)

2 Duty of 35% of their value is levied on certain goods when they are imported into this country. Find:

(a) the duty on goods valued £60; and

(b) the value of goods on which the duty is £7.84.

(L.C.C. & I. Elem., Summer 1977)

3 A certain man pays 8% of his salary into a pension fund. If his salary is £3400, how much does he pay into the pension fund? If

he pays £216 into the pension fund, how much salary did he receive?

(L.C.C. & I. Elem., Spring 1977)

4 A man borrowed £4500 for 60 days at 7½% per annum. Calculate, to the nearest penny, how much interest he had to pay (assume 1 year = 365 days).

(R.S.A. 1, March 1978)

5 A certain carpet is made in rolls 0.75 metres wide, and costs £4.50 for a metre length. Find the cost of:
(a) a strip of this carpet 0.75 metres wide and 3.4 metres long; and of
(b) carpeting a room 4.5 metres wide and 8 metres long.

(L.C.C. & I. Elem., Summer 1977)

6 A man's electricity meter readings in units for one quarter were as follows:

Beginning of quarter – 47613
End of quarter – 49204

He is charged 2.165p per unit plus a quarterly standing charge of £2.18. Calculate, to the nearest penny, his electricity bill for the quarter.

(R.S.A. 1, March 1978)

7 A man estimates that the cost of running his car for one year is made up as follows: tax £50, insurance £65, repairs £80, depreciation £550 and petrol at 78p a gallon. He travels 12000 miles a year, and his car averages 30 miles per gallon. Calculate:
(a) the total cost of the year's motoring, including depreciation; and
(b) using the answer to (a), the average cost per mile to the nearest 1/10p.

(R.S.A. 1, March 1978)

8 The rateable value of a man's house is £360. He pays £99.90 half-yearly in rates. What rate in the £ is he being charged?

(R.S.A.1, November 1977)

9 The rateable value of a town is £27,460,000. If the amount to be raised from the rates is £17,550,000, what rate in the £ will have to be levied? (give your answer to the nearest 1/10p).

(R.S.A.1, March 1978)

10 What is the equivalent price in pence per lb of food costing 16.83 francs per kilogram? (Take 1 kg = 2.2 lb, £1 = 8.5 francs.)

(R.S.A.1, November 1977)

11 A retailer purchases 100 identical shirts for a total cost of £700. He sells 64 of them at 25% profit each on cost price. At what price must he sell each of the rest of the shirts in order that his total gain will be 34% of his outlay?

(R.S.A.2, June 1977)

12 The cost of house insurance is as follows:

The house itself	£1.25 per £1000
Contents	£2.80 per £1000
Personal effects	£0.75 per £100
Contents of deep freeze	£5.50
Loss of credit cards	£1.50
5% discount on premiums above £40	

I wish to insure: my £19000 house, its contents valued at £6000, personal effects worth £800 and the possible loss of my credit cards. For what amount should I write a cheque to cover these values?

(R.S.A.2, March 1978)

13 On returning from a holiday abroad a man has 2200 pesetas and 75 francs to change back to sterling. How much sterling will he receive if the rates of exchange are:

£1 = 120 pesetas
and £1 = 8.50 francs?

(R.S.A., C.O.S., June 1977)

14 A car is bought second-hand for £690 by hire-purchase. A deposit of one-third is paid at the time of purchase and interest is charged on the balance at 20% per annum for the full period of repayment. The balance plus interest is repaid over two years in 24 monthly instalments. Calculate, to the nearest penny, the amount of each instalment.

(R.S.A., C.O.S., June 1977)

BUSINESS EDUCATION COUNCIL

General Awards

Specimen Examination Paper for
BUSINESS CALCULATIONS – MODULE 2

INSTRUCTIONS TO THE CANDIDATE

Section A

You should attempt to answer ALL QUESTIONS.
It is suggested that you spend no more than 1 hour on this section.

Section B

You should attempt to answer TWO QUESTIONS.
Allow time to study all the information before you answer any question and leave time at the end to check your answers.

You may use a battery powered, non-programmeable calculator.

ALL working calculations leading to your final answer MUST be shown.

You have TWO HOURS to complete the examination.

BEC GENERAL AWARDS

BUSINESS CALCULATIONS – MODULE 2

Specimen Question Paper

SECTION A – ANSWER ALL QUESTIONS

It is suggested that you spend no more than 1 hour on this section.

1. Calculate the cost of 1 lb of coffee if 3½ lbs cost £13.58.
2. Express (i) 5432 mm in metres; (ii) 2.5 kg in grammes
3. Find the cost of 4½ gallons of petrol at 74p per gallon
4. Rewrite as percentages (i) 0.75; (ii) 0.025

5. Rewrite as fractions (i) 27½%; (ii) 33 ⅓%
6. Calculate the area of a rectangle 3.5m long by 2.6m wide
7. Rewrite correct to 2 decimal places (i) 1.459; (ii) 3.697
8. Rewrite correct to 3 significant figures (i) 39760; (ii) 4.542
9. Calculate 7½% of £50
10. Express 45p as a percentage of £2.00
11. The postal clerk is paid £1.18 an hour, for his 40-hour week, and time and one half for overtime. What is his gross pay in a week which he works 46 hours?
12. One of your representatives required $500 expenses for a visit to a Trade Exhibition in Miami. If the rate of exchange is £1 = $1.81, calculate, to the nearest penny, how much this represents in £'s sterling.
13. A businessman estimates that each £1 received from the sale of one of his products is used as follows:

	£
Raw material	0.45
Wages and salaries	0.35
Miscellaneous costs	0.10
Profit	0.10
	£1.00

Represent this information as a pie chart.

14. Five-litre cans of golden syrup cost a grocer £2.50 a can and he sells them for £4.25. What percentage profit does he make when calculated on the selling price?
15. The weekly wages of seven girls in a typing pool are £44, £42, £41, £34, £37, £42, £42. Calculate the arithmetical mean, the median and the mode of the wages.

SECTION B – ANSWER TWO QUESTIONS

QUESTION 1

Henry Lever & Sons Ltd employs craftsmen in two different trades – Fitters and Instrument Mechanics – at factories in Slough and Welwyn. The numbers of men employed in each trade, their weekly average earnings and their place of employment are given in the following table:

	SLOUGH		WELWYN	
Trade	No. of men	Average earnings (£)	No. of men	Average earnings (£)
Fitter	40	72	48	75
Instrument Mechanic	14	85	18	91

From the information given in the table you are required to find the following:

(a) The number of men employed
 i) in each trade
 ii) at each factory
 iii) in total

(b) The total earnings
 i) in each trade
 ii) at each factory separately
 iii) at both factories together

(c) The arithmetic mean earnings for each trade taken separately.

QUESTION 2

The Time Card below shows the 'clock-on' and 'clocking-off' time for one week for Mr T Smith, an engineering fitter.

A B ENGINEERING Co.

Time Card

Name: T Smith — Week Ending: 12 May 1978
Works No. 64 — Department: Machine Shop

	AM		PM	
	IN	OUT	IN	OUT
Monday	8.00	12.00	13.00	17.00
Tuesday	7.58	12.01	12.55	17.02
Wednesday	8.13	12.01	12.59	19.00
Thursday	7.59	12.02	13.05	19.30
Friday	8.00	12.01	13.00	17.01

You are required to prepare a statement showing his gross wage, deductions and net wage for the week. The following information is relevant:

i) The basis working week is 40 hours from 8.00–12.00 and from 13.00–17.00 each day.

ii) If overtime is worked there is a tea-break from 17.00–17.30 and overtime at time plus a quarter is paid from 17.30.

iii) Mr Smith's normal rate of pay is £1.84 per hour.

iv) If more than 10 minutes late in the morning or at lunch time, a ¼ hour's pay is deducted, and a further ¼ hour for each subsequent 15 minutes late.

v) Income tax for the week is £9.45.

vi) National Insurance is calculated at 6½% of gross pay.

vii) A trade union weekly subscription of 35p is deducted.

QUESTION 3

a) The Manager of your company has to provide a car for use by a member of staff on firm's business. The firm can purchase its own car and pay its running costs, or alternatively, allow the member of staff to use his own car and pay him mileage allowance. To help reach a decision on this you are required to estimate the running costs, including depreciation, of a firm's car for one year, given the following information:
   i) Initial cost of car £3200
   ii) Assumed value after one year £2400
   iii) Estimated mileage covered during the year 6000
   iv) Cost of petrol 75p per gallon
   v) Consumption of petrol 30 miles per gallon
   vi) Insurance £75
   vii) Car tax £50
   viii) Repairs and servicing £120

b) Using this estimated total cost, calculate the cost per mile, giving the answer to the nearest 0.1p.

QUESTION 4

The following table lists the unit sales and unit selling prices of items sold in the menswear department of a store during one year:

	Shirts	Shoes	Socks	Suits
First half-year	440	310 pairs	600 pairs	110
Second half-year	520	315 pairs	400 pairs	100
Selling price	£5 each	£8 pair	75p pair	£45 each

CALCULATE:
a) The total turnover for the department for the year.
b) The mean monthly turnover on shirts.
c) The percentage of the department's turnover taken in the first half-year.
d) The percentage decrease in sales of socks in the second half-year compared with the first.
e) The department's stock turn if the average stock is £1600.
f) The turnover for the total store if the menswear sales account for 8% of the total.

Appendix – Solutions

Assignment No.

1 Total bills: £23.11; £21.49; £27.21; £41.43; £24.30.
Mistake? Mixed Iris for Falcon Hotel £1.25 per doz.

2

	M.G.	K.S.	M.P.	T.A.	G.S.	Total
Hire charge	£165.00	£266.00	£448.00	£572.00	£336.00	£1787.00
15% deposit	24.75	39.90	67.20	85.80	50.40	268.05
Outstanding	140.25	226.10	380.80	486.20	285.60	1518.95

	Bahama	*Viking*	*Heron*	*Dolphin*
May/June	£46.00	£39.75	£33.00	£29.50
July	52.00	44.50	37.00	32.83
August	59.67	51.50	42.40	37.33
After August	43.33	40.00	33.60	30.00

3 D. Chalk's commission should be £3.40
Milk is 10p per pint; Bread is 25p per loaf; eggs are 5p each.

	Cash due	Commission
K.D.	£47.35	£2.37
B.B.	55.35	2.77
J.A.	63.60	3.18

4

Room	Bill	V.A.T.	Total
18	£154.40	12.35	166.75
2	52.71	4.22	56.93
21	31.08	2.49	33.57
1	38.10	3.05	41.15
7	134.64	10.77	145.41
		32.88	443.81

5

	Cost	Trade discount	Total
Langham Books	£55.55	£16.67	£38.88
Lancs Books	44.55	13.37	31.18
A–Z Books	45.95	13.79	32.16
Gordon & Green	44.20	13.26	30.94
Mitchell	21.50	6.45	15.05
		£63.54	

6 Errors: cheque for cake dish should be £32.85, *not* £32.65, and cheque for vase should be £19.50, *not* £19.15.

7 Vivian's log = £(9.35 + 13.75 + 25.65 + 5.25 + 8.25 + 38.25)
= £100.50.
Michael's log = £(30.60 + 43.20 + 15.40 + 15.40 + 15.40 + 8.25 + 85.05 + 15.40)
= £228.70.
Thus the total of these is £329.20. With petrol = £94.06 the amount to the partners = £235.14.

8

	Cost	V.A.T.	Total
Boon's	£231.30	£18.50	£249.80
Melhuish	271.10	21.69	292.79
Barker & Trupp	169.65	13.57	183.22
Lorrimer	167.25	13.38	180.63
Freeman's	247.75	19.82	267.57
		£86.96	

Paperweights £89.53

9 Average height 171 cm.; median height 172 cm.

10 Items sold 18

Receipts	£4512
Cost	£3269.95
Profit	£1242.05

11 Alberto John £53.35 profit (ignoring costs of tickets and posters).
Average attendance Guys 77 Dolls 36
Net receipts £252.74

12

	Bananas	Grapes	Trout	Beef	Cream
per lb	25p	60p	98p	72p	48p
per kilo	56p	131p	215p	159p	

Smaller packet of Topaz is better value (16.875 grams per p).

Shoplifter's bill £20.04

13 Pandella Off-licence and Tim Cheng should pay 65p per cm^2
Total revenue for the *Stratford Beacon* £150.47

14

	Howard's	Grant	Prendergast	Spragg
Bills (inc. V.A.T.)	£70.69	£69.74	£19.68	£124.72

Profits	Last year	This year
Dan	£1886.70	£3063.84
Chris	£1048.16	£1702.14

15

	Family	Economy	Standard	Small
Wholesale price	60p	45p	33p	21p
Retail price	78p	59p	43p	27p

Average monthly sales £26.7th. (6 months)
£32.5th. (3 months)
Sep sales estimated £42.5th.
Economy size $2\frac{1}{7}$ times Small size

16 Option 1 £42120; 2 £35100; 3 £34645
9 goals = £1575; 28 goals = £4900

17 Seniors £44.10; Giants £90
Commission £19294.52; Best month December £214155.90

18 8.05 $42\frac{1}{3}$ mins 7.40 and 8.13 fastest, 8.22 slowest
57 km They could both travel on 7.32

Joanna Box? Study 8.22. If it costs £10.75 for a 44-minute journey, how much would it cost for a 17-minute journey? 685
¼

19 Photocopiers £3751 Swivel Chairs £2467.50
Staplers £700 Filing Cases £2058.60

20 (1) £13552 (2) Buddy £4387.46 Chuck £3133.90 Anne £2507.12 Stuart £2507.12 (3) 28% (4a) 26250 (4b) 17500

21 (1) Males 49.6% Females 50.4% In factory 88% under 27 47.8% (2) 8.1% (3) 32.6%

22

	Outstanding	Instalments	Final instalment
1	£463.05	£25.73	£25.64
2	£ 64.17	£ 5.35	£ 5.32
3	£497.25	£20.72	£20.69
4	£ 55.87	£ 9.31	£ 9.32
5	£ 17.65	£ 2.94	£ 2.95

23 (1) £180 (2) £162.50 (3) £273.60 (4) £187.62½

£21.71 over to buy dress costing £26.75

24 (1) £1108.24 (2) 72.9 litres

25 (1) Standards 30000 (July) 25000 (August)
Flatties 40000 (July) 41000 (August)
(2) £20750 (3) 1521

26 (1) 350 (2) £4615.65 (3) 76.3%

27 (1) £55.07 (2) £47.01 (3) 4.1% (4) £5200.87

28 Commission on Sale 1 should be £687.50 Sale 2 £432.50 Sale 3 £1037.50 Loss to firm would have been £141.50 Sale 4 £861.63 Sale 5 £918.75 Andy's commission for month £252.23 (after tax)

29 217500 litres of ice-cream 189000 kg of soups

30

	Chocolate Tasties	Chocolate Lingers	Tender Thoughts
Totals (000)	1562	943	411

31 Part 1 Total £3002.76 Part 2 £20087.60 Part 3 £158400

32 (1) Overtime adjustments: Abercrombie deduct 72p; Lever deduct 24p; Anderson add 68p; net deduct 28p. (2) Total overtime after tax £90.08 (3) £9.08 (4) B (5) £8.28

33 Profit £160.92 (1) 60% (2) 85.7% (3) 81.7% (4) 31% (5) 97.7%

34 (1) Target was reached end of December (2) Average balance £726.95, so interest would be £54.52.
Balance at start of July £374.14

35 Profit £174.71 Totals of assets/laibilities £2913.45 Balance of Bank a/c £1281.85

36 Net proceeds £15450.31; George £6180.13 Pamela £4635.09 Alan, David and Susan £1545.03 each.
Dr Barnado's £4914.06 Spastics £3685.55 War on Want £2457.03 King George's Fund £1228.52

Year 1 6% Year 2 6.75% Year 3 7.5% Year 4 8.5%

Gross interest on stocks £45.25 (net) £258.25 Cost of War Stock £759

37 (1) Median age 23 years Average age 25.9 years (2) Median salary £1985.25 Average salary £2348.95

(2) Females only; Median age 23 years Average age 26.7 years Median salary £1985.25 Average salary £2274.92

Tax payable p.a.; Thelma £378.30 June £184.50 Jeremy £782.90 John £293.30

38 Cost of holiday £472.74 All bargains except shaver, cigarette case and jeans.

39 Judi brings back £327.28 (1) £10.64 (2) £2048.19/£2207.79

40 Break-even = 6000+

Percentages, Fractions and Decimals – see Figure 1.1 (p. 12) but remainder as follows:

1/8 = 12½% or 0.13, 1/16 = 6¼% or 0.06, 22½% = 9/40 or 0.23, 0.03 = 3% or 3/100, 1/40 = 2½% or 0.03, 1/3 = 33 1/3% or 0.33, 1/12 = 0.08 or 8 1/3%, 2/25 = 8% or 0.08, 17½% = 7/40 or 0.18, 3/8 = 37½% or 0.38, 1.65 = 165% or 1 13/20, 1 3/8% = 11/800 or 0.01, 7/8 = 87½% or 0.88,0.01 = 1% or 1/100, 5/16 = 31¼% or 0.31, 2¾% = 11/400 or 0.03, 7/16 = 0.44 or 43¾%, 1.05 = 105% or 1 1/20, 9/16 = 56¼% or 0.56, 4 7/8% = 39/800 or 0.05, 11/16 = 68¾% or 0.69, 10.11 = 10 11/100 or 1011%, 1/32 = 3 1/8% or 0.03, 98% = 49/50 or 0.98, 3/32 = 9 3/8% or 0.09, 3.75 = 375% or 3¾.

Pick the Winner A B B C B B B B C C A B A B B B C C B B C A C

Time Trial Grand Total £1997.60

Add and Check Section A £1511.85 Section B £2657.51

Call, Copy and Add

	1	2	3	4
List A	£1675.51	£1100.75	£312.72	£176.36
List B	£166.74	£1154.85	£661.57	£39.26
	5	6	7	8
List A	£1109.13	£354.64	£129.49	£2631.88
List B	£1314.67	£166.56	£376.41	£2915.41

Multiply and Subtract Grand Total £1796.79

Divide and Add Grand Total £1864.78

Meter Readings A £489.43 B £931.66 C £266.21 D £884.98

Foreign Exchange Handicap I Section A £887.43 Section B £659.33

Foreign Exchange Handicap II Section A £30.52 5843.47 pesetas
Section B £24.94 2473.42 escudos

Convert and Compare Total £101.68

Averages

	A	B	C	D	E	F	G	H	I
Arithmetic mean	42.67	27.25	13.76	39.17	17.9	20.8	20.68	25.81	25.15
Median	16.5	22.76	9.9	25.0	11.7	9.9	8.8	17.25	16.5
Mode	16.5								

The Gladiators I Grand Total £339.74

The Gladiators II Grand Total £290.28

Debits and Credits I Final balance £355.13

Debits and Credits II Final balance £1820.79

The Satellite La Patte (4 cm^2 £658.82)

Examination Questions

1 (a) £3.60 (b) 12½%
2 (a) £21 (b) £22.40
3 £272 and £2700
4 £55.48
5 (a) £15.30 (b) £216
6 £36.63
7 (a) £1057 (b) 8⅘p
8 55p in £

9 63 9/10 p in £
10 90p per lb
11 £10.50
12 £45.65
13 £27.15
14 £26.83

BEC General Paper
Section A

1 £3.88
2 (i) 5.432 m (ii) 2500 g
3 £3.33
4 (i) 75% (ii) 2½%
5 (i) 11/40 (ii) 1/3
6 $9.1m^2$
7 (i) 1.46 (ii) 3.70
8 (i) 39800 (ii) 4.54
9 £3.75
10 22½%
11 £57.82
12 £276.24
13 162^0 126^0 36^0 36^0
14 70%
15 £40.29; £42; £42

Section B

1 (a) (i) 88 fitters; 32 mechanics (ii) 54 at Slough, 66 at Welwyn (iii) 120 in total.
(b) (i) £6480 p.w. fitters; £2828 p.w. mechanics
(ii) £4070 p.w. Slough; £5238 p.w. Welwyn
(iii) £9308 p.w.
(c) £76.64 p.w. fitters; £88.38 p.w. mechanics
2 Gross wage £81.19, deductions £15.08, net wage £66.11
3 Annual cost £1195, cost per mile 19.9p
4 (a) £20000 (b) £400 (c) 50.4% (d) 33⅓%
(e) 20000/1600 = 12.5 times p.a. (f) £250000